Housetraining

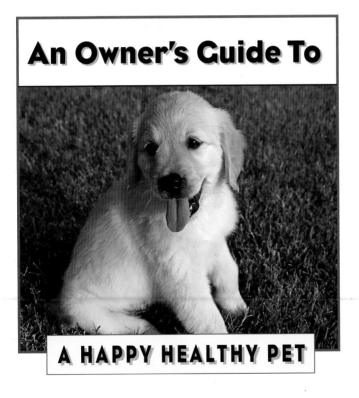

An Owner's Guide To

A HAPPY HEALTHY PET

Howell Book House

Wiley Publishing, Inc.

Library of Congress Cataloging-in-Publication Data

Morn, September B.
Housetraining / by September B. Morn; featuring photographs by Winter/Churchill/DOGPHO-
TO.COM.
    p. cm.—(An owner's guide to a happy healthy pet)
Includes bibliographical references.

ISBN 1-58245-010-2

1. Dogs—Training. 2. Puppies—Training. I. Title. II. Series.
SF431.M824   1999, 2001   98-42792
636.7'0887—dc21   CIP
Manufactured in the United States of America
10 9 8
Second Edition

Author's Note: Throughout this book, dogs are referred to as "it." This decision was made in the
interest of gender neutrality, as the majority of housetraining issues are not relevant to a dog's
gender. Of course, your dog is either a he or she and these pronouns are used when referring to a
dog of a particular gender.

Series Director: Kira Sexton
Book Design: Michele Laseau
Cover Design: Michael Freeland
Photography Editor: Richard Fox
Photography:
  Front and back cover photos supplied by Winter/Churchill/DOGPHOTO.COM
  Interior photography by Winter/Churchill/DOGPHOTO.COM
Page creation by: Wiley Indianapolis Composition Services

Contents

part one

About
Housetraining

Canine

Cleanliness

Mama Dog's Job

Six little puppies squirm and wiggle, crawling closer to their mother's warmth and sweet milk. The litter is 3 days old. The pups neither see nor hear at this young age, as their eyes and ears will not open for another week. Their sense of touch is working well though, as is their sense of smell. The puppies' tiny, pudgy noses lead them to their mama, lying ready to nurse them full and fat with her abundant milk.

Mama dog keeps a proud vigil over her six new babies, one eye on the door of the whelping room and the other on her brand-new family. The mother dog is ready to protect her babies from any possible threat.

Six puppies nurse in a row at their dam's belly. Suckling noises and grunts of satisfaction please the mama dog. She pants softly as she watches her contented brood. The largest pup releases its suction hold and furiously nuzzles around, looking for a fuller spot at mama's milk bar. The pup tumbles over two nursing littermates then finds an unoccupied position and begins to nurse again, kneading the dam's belly with tiny round paws. Once again, all is right in the pup's world.

A PUP ELIMINATES

The dam's ears twitch toward a slightly different sound. The big pup is still nursing, but its snuffling, suckling sounds have changed. Now it is making a slightly different puppy grunt. Mama's nose goes to the pup immediately. She nuzzles her baby, then gently begins to lick its belly and backside.

The pup wiggles, feeling its mother's attention, and becomes still for a moment. The stimulation of its dam's insistent lapping releases the pup's urine and feces. Without the mother's attention, new puppies are unable to eliminate their own body wastes. The mother's licking is vital to the pup's survival.

The mama dog cleans up her pup's wastes as it produces them, then washes the pup from head to toe, removing every trace of odor. She then repeats this with each pup in turn until all have relieved themselves and been cleaned. The dam tidies her whelping nest until it once again is spotless. Then she relaxes and naps for a short time with her clean, contented brood.

Early Development

The puppies sleep away 90 percent of their first two weeks of life, waking only to nurse and be cleaned. Their dark and quiet world is informed through their senses of smell and touch. Unable to control their own body temperature, the pups spend most of their time huddled together or cuddled against their dam.

At about 18 days of age, the pups develop the physical coordination and strength to progress from a belly crawl to a shaky walk. One of the first journeys a puppy takes is a few steps away from the sleeping corner to eliminate. Even very young puppies seem to know instinctively that it's improper to soil their sleeping and eating quarters.

By about 3 weeks of age, the pups have gained some control over their own elimination. They no longer require the stimulation of their mother's insistent licking. They can "go" on their own, although mama still nurses them and cleans up their body waste.

At first, the mother stays with her puppies around the clock, leaving them only when she must eat or relieve herself. As the pups grow, they become mobile and curious. They start to follow their mama when she leaves the whelping nest. A few steps away from the clean sleeping area, the mama dog stops. The pups, close behind her, also stop. They try to nurse, but mama won't allow it. The pups mill around in frustration, then nature calls and they all urinate and defecate here, away from their bed. The dam returns to the nest with her toddler brood waddling behind her. Their first potty training lesson has been a success.

During the first few weeks of life, mama dog stays with her puppies all day.

Now about 5 weeks old, the pups are mobile and active, although a bit clumsy. They are beginning to play games of tag and "stalking" with each other and their dam. Their eyesight and hearing are good now. The sound of one puppy nursing brings the other five scrambling to dinner.

The pups' sharp little teeth are now in and this begins to annoy their dam. The pin-pointed puppy teeth are rough on her sensitive teats. The hungry litter, dining so vigorously, is becoming painful to her. Weaning time has arrived.

The Breeder's Job

When the pups are about 4 to 5 weeks of age they are growing too fast to be satisfied with mother's milk. The breeder begins to supplement their diet with puppy food, softened to a slurpy gruel. The pups lap up this mixture hungrily, pushing and shoving one another, sliding around in the slippery mush that fills the flat communal feeding dish. When the puppies have finished dinner, they take dessert by licking smears of leftover gruel from each other's fur.

CLEANLINESS

Mama dog's job of feeding and mopping up after her brood is nearly finished at this point. The babies are no longer dependent on her milk, as their tiny sharp teeth are ready to chew solid food. Once puppies begin eating solids, their dam no longer laps up their body waste. The pups still need their mother to teach them important rules and customs of dog society, but the breeder now must take over their feeding and hygiene.

The breeder keeps the puppies clean and their living area sanitary by frequent and thorough housekeeping. Having planned far ahead for this litter's birth, the breeder has saved the local daily newspaper for several months and has asked friends to save theirs for him as well. He opens sections of the clean newspaper and spreads them thickly wall-to-wall in the pups' corner to catch and absorb puppy piddles and water spills.

As the breeder places the layers of newspaper on the puppies' floor, he removes all the shiny advertising inserts. These are slippery under the pups' feet and have little absorbency. Also, the brightly colored ink in the ads sometimes contains pigment derived from toxic metals, and a careful breeder protects puppies from accidentally ingesting those poisons.

Earliest Potty Training

Although the puppies are eating solids, their dam still nurses them several times a day. Her milk supply is lessening, though, and the pups are growing bigger and hungrier. Mama usually leaves the den area immediately after she suckles her pups. The breeder has securely placed a board across the entrance to the puppy corner. Mama can easily hop over this barrier, but it is too high for the pups to follow her.

They run after their dam as she leaves, hoping for just a bit more of her sweet milk, but she disappears over the barrier board. The pups mill around in frustration for a moment, then feel urgency in their bladders and bowels. The whole litter eliminates together. The pups then return to their sleeping corner to play for a few minutes before they all settle down for an after-dinner nap.

The breeder watches as the puppies eliminate, then deftly removes the soiled papers and replaces them with clean papers before they

The breeder starts the housetraining process early by providing a paper-covered area for the puppies.

can traipse back through their messes. He has wisely arranged the puppy space so their bed, food and drinking water are as far away from the gate as possible. This way, when the pups follow their mama as she leaves them after suckling, they will move away from their sleeping and eating area before eliminating. This helps strengthen the natural canine habit of keeping the inner den clean of body waste. Once formed, this habit will help the pups be readily housetrained when adopted into their permanent homes.

POTTY OUTDOORS

As the puppies grow bigger and more energetic, the breeder decides to allow them to go outside for short periods in suitable weather. The pups play and romp and wrestle with each other. They work up a thirst and quench it with fresh water from a bowl the breeder keeps filled for them in their outdoor playpen. One pup feels nature's call and walks to the edge of the play area to pee. Several other pups notice and realize that they too have to go. They urinate near the spot where the first pup went.

These puppies are accustomed to a clean den because their living space has been kept sanitary and relatively odor free, first by their dam and then their breeder. The lack of odor and mess teaches the pups not to soil their sleeping and eating areas. They learn to move as far away as they can from the nest before squatting to potty. Soon these pups will go to their new homes, where proud owners will be delighted with how quickly the pups understand and obey household cleanliness rules.

The Owner's Job

The day arrives for the puppy buyer to bring her new family member home. She is excited as she prepares to drive to the breeder's facility two hours distant. She remembers to bring the rubber bone she bought at the pet supply store yesterday while purchasing the items her new pup would need upon arrival.

The buyer loads a puppy-sized crate into the front seat and buckles the seat belt securely around it. She checks the map and the directions the breeder sent, then makes certain she has some bottled water for the pup.

Everything's ready to go. Well, almost—at the last minute she returns to the kitchen to grab spray cleaner, a roll of paper towels and a big plastic trash bag for the inevitable spills, leaks, puppy piddles and car sickness.

**MARKING A
POTTY SPOT
FOR YOUR NEW DOG**

While you're at your pup's old home, obtain a paper towel with some urine on it from your pup or its littermates. Put this in a plastic bag and take it home with you. Place the soiled paper towel on the ground in the area where you want your pup to eliminate. Pour $1/2$ cup of water through the towel onto the ground, to mark the spot, scenting the new potty area with urine. This will give your pup the clue it needs to understand where to eliminate at its new home.

GETTING THE NEW PUP

As the buyer turns into the breeder's driveway, an adult dog barks and the breeder opens his front door and waves. Two puppies snoozing in the shade in a clean, grassy pen awaken and run to the fence to see who has arrived.

The puppies place their little feet up on the fence and lick the buyer's fingers through the wire mesh. The pup reserved for the buyer is wearing a green nylon collar, the other puppy's collar is red. The green-collared puppy suddenly stops licking and gets down from the fence, walks a few steps away, sniffs and urinates. The buyer notices that the puppies' pen is very clean, she sees only one poop—right next to where the pup just eliminated.

After a flurry of final details, the new owner is ready to leave for home with her furry little family member. The breeder has given her a sheaf of papers, including registration paperwork, immunization records and instructions for feeding and care. He also sends along a week's supply of the food the pup is used to eating.

The breeder nods in approval when he sees the new owner has brought a crate to safely transport the pup home. She loads the pup into the crate and checks the seat belt to be sure it is fastened securely.

A new owner will want to scent a spot with the puppy's urine so as to create a potty spot.

THE TRIP HOME

The puppy settles down in the crate, happily chewing on the rubber bone. For the first few miles the pup occasionally gets restless and whines. After that, it settles down and sleeps for about half an hour. When the puppy wakes and starts to cry again, the new owner decides that it's time for a potty break. She pulls into a rest stop and clips a lightweight leash to the pup's collar; it would be too dangerous to walk the pup off-lead here, so close to traffic.

A Potty Stop

Be prepared to take your puppy out to its potty spot frequently during the first few weeks of its life in its new home.

The owner carries her pup to a likely spot and sets it on the ground. The puppy sits and scratches at its collar, then gets up and starts to sniff, turns half a circle and pees. Success! The owner waits a few minutes more, just in case the pup isn't finished. Sure enough, it goes again. Then they hit the road. The pup soon falls asleep in the crate again and the trip is uneventful.

The New Home

The owner marks the potty spot and takes the puppy there to relieve itself. Success— times two! Afterward, she brings the puppy back inside, into the kitchen, where already set up is a baby-gated puppy corral with newspaper on the floor.

As she prepares supper, she keeps an eye on the pup playing around her feet. After a while she feeds the pup, placing its dinner bowl in the far corner of the kitchen, next to its crate/bed and tip-proof water bowl.

After the pup finishes eating, the owner takes it out to the potty area. The pup relieves itself immediately. The owner praises the puppy and gives herself a mental pat on the back for preparing for all of this ahead of time. She begins to realize that housetraining this puppy is probably going to be easier than she had anticipated.

Teach—Don't Punish!

The foregoing situation was ideal: The dam was a good mother and teacher, the breeder was knowledgeable and the new owner was prepared. From the beginning the odds were stacked in favor of the pup's success. The dam started her pup's housetraining education, the breeder furthered it and the new owner continued in a way that helped the pup succeed. If every breeder and new owner did their homework as thoroughly as in our story, there would be very few problems with housetraining.

PUNISHMENT IS INEFFECTIVE

Punishment is not an effective tool for housetraining most dogs. Many will react to punishment by hiding puddles and poop where the owner won't find them right away (like behind the couch or under the desk). This eventually may lead to punishment after the fact, which leads to more pee and poop hiding, etc.

Instead of punishing for mistakes, stay a step ahead of potty accidents by learning to anticipate your pup's needs. Know your pup's schedule—its body rhythms will let you know when elimination time should be coming. Learn to recognize your pup's body language; its postures and actions when it's getting ready to urinate or defecate. Accompany your dog to the designated potty area when it needs to go. Tell it what you want it to do; teach it a command to eliminate. Wait patiently with your pup and then praise it when it goes. This will work wonders. Punishment won't be necessary if you are a good teacher.

In life, there are challenges. Housetraining a puppy or adult dog can be one of them, but there are things you can do to make it easier. Often, all that's needed to prevent or solve elimination problems is a little experienced guidance and a few new tricks. This book is written to provide you with both. When you understand your dog's needs and natural inclinations, housetraining it will be no problem.

Getting Ready
for Your
New Dog

When you have all the essentials in place before your dog arrives, it will be easier to help it adjust to your household rules. It's wise to acquire the tools and information needed for success at any new task. House-training a dog is no exception to the rule. Before bringing your new companion home, you should prepare for its arrival. This means doing some planning and probably some shopping.

Supplies, equipment, and setup will vary somewhat, depending on the age of the new dog and its previous housetraining experience. A young pup will demand more of the owner's time and attention and need to eliminate more often than an older pup or adult. Puppies may also require more supplies, especially for clean-up chores. Be sure

14

you have plenty of everything you'll need to start your
dog off right.

Equipment and Supplies

What's black and white and wet all over? This riddle is
easy for new puppy owners. That's right, newspaper!

NEWSPAPER

Reusing newspaper was popular
among dog breeders and puppy
owners long before recycling be-
came a household word. A tall stack
of newspapers is a handy resource
for anyone trying to housetrain a
puppy. Be sure to have plenty on
hand. The rule on sufficient newspaper supply is: The younger your
puppy and larger its breed, the
more newspapers you'll need.

Newspaper has many virtues. It is absorbent, abundant, cheap and convenient. A section of the average
daily news can soak up a rather
large puddle.

NEWSPAPER INK TOXICITY

Years ago, the ink used for printing newspapers contained lead
and other toxic metals that were
dangerous if ingested. Today, most
newspapers are printed with non-
toxic vegetable-based inks. Some
of the colorful advertising inserts,
however, may still be printed with
metal pigments so to be on the safe
side, don't use those pages for
puppy potty papers. The black-and-
white sections are not only safer,
they're more absorbent.

PUDDLE PADS

If you prefer not to stockpile newspaper, a commercial
alternative is available. Thick paper pads backed with
a sheet of plastic can be purchased under several trade
names at pet supply stores. These puddle pads have the
advantage of being waterproof so puppy urine doesn't
seep through onto the floor. Their disadvantages are
that they will cost you more than newspapers and that
they contain plastics that are not biodegradable.

Cleanup Supplies

An essential for potty training is a good supply of paper
towels and spray cleaner. Immediately washing away
all puppy accidents will help prevent your dog from

returning to those spots to soil again. Dogs mark their territory with their own unique scent by depositing urine and feces in strategic locations. Any dog can tell with a simple sniff whose turf it's entering. Detecting the scent of its own or another dog's urine, a dog may mark that spot repeatedly.

CLEANING PRODUCTS

Enzyme preparations and special cleaners that make urine scent less detectable to dogs are available at pet supply stores. Some owners find that using vinegar after cleaning with household spray diminishes or masks the smell of dog urine. Before using any unfamiliar cleaning product on carpet or fabric, test on a small area to be sure it doesn't stain or bleach.

Thorough cleaning to remove the scent of a potty mistake in your house will decrease the likelihood that your dog will mark that spot again. The scent of urine can be very difficult to eradicate. Low-power human noses may be satisfied the smell is gone after spray cleaning, but enough scent may linger that your dog's nose can find it.

Picking Up

To maintain sanitation and pleasant surroundings, a dog's potty area must be kept clean. This job should be done daily. Not only does daily pickup prevent the chore from becoming overwhelming, it allows the dog owner to visually check the dog's droppings on a regular basis. Why would anyone want to do that? For health's sake—the dog's, that is. Keeping track of your dog's bowel movements can give early warnings about several serious health problems. Fortunately, most conditions causing abnormal stools can be remedied if detected at an early stage.

Clean up accidents right away so as to leave no scent behind.

Picking up poop is a chore many dog owners put off—obviously because they dislike doing it. One reason owners procrastinate is because they have the wrong tool for the job. People often try to use a garden shovel to pick up dog droppings, which is clumsy, difficult and unpleasant. The angle of a shovel handle forces the dog owner to bend forward, placing the face directly over the mess. Ick! A much better solution is to use a specially manufactured dog waste scoop.

Poop Removal at Home

Several brands of poop removal tools are available. Some are designed with a pan and rake on two separate handles, and others with the handles hinged like scissors. Some scoops need two hands for operation, while others are designed for one-handed use. Experienced dog owners usually favor one style over another. Try a dry run with different brands at your pet supply store. Put a handful of pebbles or dog kibble on the floor and then pick them up with each type of scoop to determine which type works best for you. Yard scooping is much less unpleasant when you use the right tool.

An in-ground dog waste digester can make life with a dog more pleasant. This device consists of a container buried in the ground, with a lid on top to keep weather out and odors in. If you can dig a hole in your yard, you can install one of these simple devices. Special enzymes are periodically poured over the droppings in the container to speed decomposition. The dog droppings are converted into soil and more or less disappear. Many dog owners find these digesters help keep the yard insect- and odor-free.

Public Courtesy

When you and your dog friend take walks together, you'll need another poop-scooping accessory: plastic bags. Dog waste is unsightly, smelly and can harbor disease. In many cities and towns, the law mandates dog owners clean up pet waste deposited on public ground. These are good laws, but too many dog owners ignore them. For some reason, many people are negligent about cleaning up after their dogs in public. This gives all dog owners a bad name. Nothing turns community sentiment against dogs and dog owners faster than piles of poop in parks and other public places. It's our responsibility as dog owners to always clean up after our canine pals.

Picking up after your dog using a plastic bag scoop is simple. Just put your hand inside the bag, like a mitten, then grab up the droppings. Turn the bag inside out, tie the top, and that's that. It's not very aesthetic, but it gets the job done. Cleaning up after our dogs is a responsibility that must be taken seriously if we hope to keep our public dog-walking privileges intact.

There is probably no way to turn poop pickup on dog walks into a recreational favorite, but there is a way to make it quick and easy. Several companies sell special bags for cleaning up, some of which have a cardboard hoe with a plastic bag attached, others have cardboard jaws. Some are scented with perfume, others are plain. Whatever the design, the object is to scoop doggie droppings into a bag to be carried home or tossed into a convenient garbage can.

There is no need for designer poop-scoop bags, so long as you clean up after your dog.

Many dog owners find that ordinary plastic bags from the grocery store work just as well as fancier scoop bags. One-gallon food storage bags are a good size and can be purchased inexpensively in boxes of 50 to 100. Some people reuse plastic produce bags for poop pickup. If you recycle bags this way, be sure to check for holes first.

WASTE DISPOSAL

A conscientious pet owner takes care of his neighborhood as well as his pet. Check your local laws concerning disposal of animal waste. Some cities ban dog and cat feces from household garbage. Others have special guidelines for disposal. If dumping pet droppings in the trash is not permitted in your town, find out how to legally dispose of them.

Potty Bell

One very special piece of equipment will make housetraining easier for both you and your dog. That object is a bell on a cord. Hang this bell at dog nose level from the handle of the door you use for taking your pup out to eliminate. Ring the bell each time you take your dog to potty. The sound of the bell soon becomes linked in the dog's mind with the opening of that door. Before long, it will try ringing the bell itself, hoping to make the door open.

When you hear that bell ring, come a-runnin'! Praise your dog and open the door.

A good potty bell can be a single bell on a string or a few attached to a strip of cloth or leather. Be sure the bell is loud enough to hear from a room or two away. If your dog rings, and you don't arrive to open the door, it may give up. Ringing the potty bell to go outside is one of the best tricks a dog can know.

Confining Your Pup

To housetrain a puppy, you will need some way to confine it when you're unable to supervise. With one or more baby gates, a folding exercise pen and a dog crate, you'll be able to socialize your pup while keeping it out of trouble.

Baby Gates

Be sure the baby gates you use are safe. The old-fashioned, wooden, expanding lattice type of gate has seriously injured a number of children by collapsing and trapping a leg, arm or neck. That type of gate can hurt a puppy, too, so use the modern grid type gates instead. You'll need more than one baby gate if you have several doorways to close off.

Exercise Pens

Portable exercise pens are great when you have a young pup or small dog. These metal or plastic pens are made of rectangular panels that are hinged together. The pens are freestanding, sturdy, foldable and can be carried like a suitcase. You could set one up in your kitchen as the pup's daytime corral, and then take it outdoors to contain your pup while you garden or just sit and enjoy the day.

Crates

A dog crate or travel kennel is a secure way to confine your dog for short periods during the day and to use as a comfortable bed at night. Some people look at a dog crate and immediately think, "cage." Many dogs are suspicious of crates at first, but readily learn to like them. A dog will consider its crate a pleasant private room of its own.

OVERUSE OF A CRATE

A crate serves well as a dog's overnight bed, but you should not leave the dog in its crate for long hours during the day. Throughout the day, the dog needs to play and exercise. It is likely to want to drink some water and will undoubtedly eliminate. Confining your dog all day will give it no option but to soil its crate. This is not just unpleasant for you and the dog, but it reinforces bad cleanliness habits.

Crates come in wire mesh and in plastic. The wire type has the advantage of being foldable to store flat in a smaller space. The plastic type has the advantages of being cozy, draft-free, quiet, and safety approved for air travel.

A crate is a cozy bed for a dog and a valuable housetraining aid. Most dogs will not ordinarily soil their bedding. Proper use of a crate can help your dog learn to hold its bladder and bowels for gradually increasing periods.

A dog's crate provides it with its own cozy place and serves as a valuable housetraining aid.

Home Setup

A dog needs many of the same things we do to be comfortable and healthy. Pups and people both need a place to eat, sleep, play or work, and a place to eliminate. Homes and lifestyles vary and each dog is unique, so each housetraining situation is a little bit different.

Look around your living space. How is it set up inside? What is it like outside? Is there an easily accessible spot that can serve as your dog's toilet area? The ideal situation might include a yard that could be fenced to allow the dog to play and lounge safely, but that's not always the case. Not everyone has a yard, and not every yard can be fenced. There is almost always a way, though, to arrange your pup's area so the housetraining process will be made easier.

INDOOR SETUP

A pup or dog that has not finished housetraining should never—repeat—never be allowed the run of the house unattended. A new dog (especially a pup) with unlimited access to your house will, through no fault of its own, wreak havoc. If you let your pup or new dog roam your home without watching its every move, puddles and piles will follow in its wake. Prevention is the most efficient solution. Prevent problems by setting up a controlled environment for your new pet.

Socialization Considerations

A good place for a puppy's home base is usually the kitchen. Set up your pup's playpen corral there if possible. Kitchens almost always have waterproof or easily cleaned floors, which is a distinct asset with leaky pups. A bathroom, laundry room or enclosed porch could be used for a puppy corral, but the kitchen is generally the best location. Kitchens are a meeting place and hub of activity for many families. A puppy will learn better manners when socialized thoroughly with family, friends and nice strangers. Without sufficient social and mental stimulation, a pup may develop inappropriate shyness, aggression and bad habits, such as barking and destructive chewing. Corralled in the kitchen, a pup will become accustomed to many sounds, sights and smells, learn approved behavior and won't become lonely or bored.

Protecting Your Home

If your kitchen is small, a baby gate blocking the doorway can turn it into a fine puppy corral. If the kitchen is large, you may find a portable exercise pen will work better for your pup. An exercise pen has the advantage of making it difficult (nothing's impossible) for a pup to chew on your kitchen cabinets.

The kitchen makes a great spot for a puppy's corral— the floors are easily cleaned and the pup will get to spend time with you.

Even with vinyl flooring, you might wish to further protect your kitchen from puddles and other puppy damage. This can be done by first putting down a piece of heavy plastic sheeting, then a sheet of plywood. On top of the plywood, you can then spread your newspapers for the pup. This extra protection can be removed once your pup is housetrained.

Protecting Your Pup

Pups are incredibly curious and will eat almost anything they can find. Keep this in mind as you puppy-proof all the areas where your pup will spend time alone. Floor-level kitchen cabinets, especially those under the sink, often hold caustics and other poisons.

Electrical cords are a common danger for pups; chewing one can have fatal results. Plug your appliances into counter-high outlets if you can, or blockade the pup's access to plugs near the floor. Make certain that no cords dangle temptingly. Your pup might tug one and pull a hot or heavy appliance down onto itself.

Check and then double check for dangers. Remove any harmful objects that your pup might get into.

When you think you've cleared away all the hazards, get down on your hands and knees to puppy eye-level and take another look. You may be surprised at how different things appear from a dog's angle.

Layout of Pup's Area

The way you structure your pup's area is very important. Remember back to the whelping nest and the puppy's early experiences and natural inclinations. The bed, food and water should be at the opposite end of the pup's corral from its potty area. If you will be training your dog to eliminate outside, place its indoor potty papers at the end of the corral closest to the door that leads to the outdoor potty. That way as it moves away from the clean area to the toilet area the pup will also form the habit of heading toward the door to go out.

Paper a large area for a new puppy. With time, you can decrease the size of the papered area.

When you first get your pup, spread newspaper over the whole floor of its playpen corral. Lay the papers at least four pages thick and be sure to overlap the edges. As you note the pup's progress away from food and bed to go potty, you can remove the papers nearest the sleeping/eating corner. Gradually decrease the size of the papered area until only the end where you want the pup to eliminate is covered. Keep the papers neatly squared for best results. Sloppy, ragged-edged potty-papered areas do not encourage the pup to be neat. Be sure to leave enough target papers that the pup doesn't accidentally miss and wet the floor.

The Importance of Scent

Maintain a scent marker for the pup's potty area by reserving a small soiled piece of its paper when you clean up. Place this piece, with its scent of urine, under the top sheet of the clean papers you spread. This will cue your pup where to eliminate. When the pup needs to go potty, it will search around for the scent and find that hidden trace of odor. You would barely be able to smell it yourself, but your pup will have no trouble at all finding the right spot.

Outdoor Setup

Fences are safer for dogs than tie-outs. Unfortunately, though, at times a fence is not an option and some other form of confinement must be used. Plastic-covered metal cable is safer than chain and cannot be chewed through as easily as rope. A tie-out fastened just outside your door is handy to clip your dog to when it needs to eliminate. For your convenience, the cable should be reachable from the doorway so you can let your dog in and out without having to leave the house. Save yourself and your pup some misery and don't put its tie-out where it can tangle around bushes, trees or lawn furniture.

TIE-OUTS

An overhead trolley tie-out tangles less than other types and is probably the safest tethering option, but these too have caused injury and death to unattended dogs. Be aware that tying or chaining a dog can be very dangerous. A dog can become fatally entangled in its rope or cable. If you use the tie-out only for the time it takes your dog to eliminate, you will probably have no serious problems, but your dog should never be tied and then left alone.

FENCES

Perhaps you are one of the fortunate dog owners with a yard or patio that can be safely enclosed as an outdoor space for your pup. If this is the case, try to arrange your setup so you can let your pup out into its fenced play yard directly from its indoor corral area. A fenced yard immediately accessible from the pup's indoor area will greatly facilitate the housetraining process. The more rooms you must pass through between the indoor corral and the outdoor potty, the more difficult it will be for your pup. You might even consider installing a doggie door so your pup can let itself in and out at will.

LAYOUT OF PUP'S YARD

When setting up your pup's outdoor yard, put the lounging area as far as possible away from the toilet area, just as with the indoor corral setup. Be sure to pick up droppings at least once a day. Leave just one poop in the potty area to remind your dog where the right spot is. If too many piles litter the ground, your dog won't want to walk through it and will start eliminating elsewhere. Dogs have a natural desire to stay far away from their own excrement; forcing a dog to live in its poop is not just unpleasant, it's cruel.

A fenced yard that is easy for your pup to get to is a bonus in successful housetraining.

Although most dogs enjoy spending time outdoors, they should not have to live there. Many dogs are forced by unknowledgeable owners to live lonely lives in kennel runs or tied to a doghouse outside. These dogs may know no other life, but they suffer from their loneliness. Dogs are social creatures. They need people, dog friends, activity, training and play. Isolation causes dysfunctional behavior patterns, such as excessive barking, digging and overaggression.

Bring your dog into your home when you're there. Give it quality attention every day. The more time your dog spends with you, the better behaved, smarter and more enjoyable companion it will be.

Bringing
Your New Dog
Home

The Homecoming

At last the big day has arrived! It's time to bring home your new dog. You've been carefully preparing for the arrival of the pup. A potty yard is fenced outside and your kitchen is baby-gated as a puppy corral, with a comfortable dog crate, tip-proof water bowl and several safe chew toys. Your cupboards are filled with high-quality dog food.

CRATE FOR TRAVEL

As you're about to walk out the door you remember to grab that new dog crate from the kitchen to take with you for the pup to ride in on the way home. Whether or not your new dog is crate-trained, it will be safer riding in a crate. Inside its new crate-den, the dog will be less distracting to the driver and won't create dangerous situations.

At first your pup might object to a crate if it's never been in one before. It's natural for dogs to resist unfamiliar situations. Give it something yummy to chew while in the crate and the pup will worry less about being confined.

A plastic crate is usually best for car travel because it's strength and rigidity protect the dog in case of sudden stops and turns. Plastic crates have solid sides that don't rattle like the wire type, so they are more cozy and quiet for the dog. With a plastic crate, if the pup goes potty or gets carsick on the way home, the mess won't leak out of the crate and soil your car.

TRAVEL GEAR

A crate for a pup or small dog will fit on the seat of most cars. If you're transporting your dog alone, place the crate in the front seat and strap it in with the seat belt. Face the door of the crate toward you, so your puppy can watch you drive instead of viewing the scenery whizzing toward the windshield. Doing so can help prevent puppy motion sickness. If you have an assistant with you, secure the crate in the back seat and have your helper sit with the pup to keep it content.

You'll need a large bag to stow all the gear your pup will require on a car trip. Parents of young children sling along a diaper bag stuffed with kid equipment wherever they go. Packing puppy necessities is similar. Your doggie bag should hold a leash, flashlight, quart of drinking water, biscuits or dry dog kibble, small pull-open can of dog food, spare chew toys, plastic bags for poop pick up, a roll of paper towels and a first-aid kit with supplies for people and pets. Truly prepared dog owners also keep in the car some spray cleaner, old towels and a package of disposable wet wipes for hand cleaning. Toting a few extra things you might not use is better than being caught without needed supplies.

SCENT MARK

When you are adopting your new dog, obtain a bit of newspaper or paper towel soiled with some of its urine. If your pup is still with its littermates, a scrap of newspaper from their communal potty area will do the trick. Carry this scented paper home to mark the area you've chosen as your pup's elimination place. If the dog smells its own urine in the potty area at its new home, it should adapt more readily to using that spot.

If your home is more than an hour from where you adopt your dog, its first lesson in elimination manners will be on the drive home. Stop for a potty break after about thirty or forty minutes of travel, sooner if the dog is restless. It's normal for a pup to fuss a bit if it's never been on a car ride, but if after fifteen minutes your dog still won't settle, it may need to eliminate.

ELIMINATION BREAK

When you stop, leash your dog before you let it out of the car. It's not at all safe or wise to allow a new dog to run free. It doesn't know you yet and you really don't know it either. Don't give it a chance to run off and get lost or injured. Leash it instead.

Allow the dog a chance to walk around and stretch its legs. It

On the way home from the breeder's (or anytime that you are traveling with your dog), take a break to let it eliminate and to stretch its legs.

may need to urinate or defecate, so allow ample opportunity for that. After it eliminates, walk the pup around or just talk to it and pet it. The bonding process has begun and although you may have met the pup only hours ago, right now you are the most familiar face in its universe. Let everything you do show your new dog you're its trustworthy friend and will care for its needs.

After your potty and petting break, return to the area where your pup eliminated earlier and calmly encourage it to go again. It may or it may not need to, but offer it the chance. After a minute or so, load everyone in the car again and head for home.

The First Day—First Impressions Are Lasting

The first day with a new dog is a very exciting time for the whole family. The pup has met you, but on arriving home everyone will be excited to pet and play with it. Keep an eye on the puppy and take it to the potty place before it can have accidents on the floor.

When you arrive home, take the urine marked paper you brought from your pup's former home and rub the scent in the area(s) that you've selected as elimination places for your new dog. If you'll be training the pup to potty outdoors, pour ½ cup of water through the urine paper and let it seep into the ground there. Don't leave the paper on the ground though, or your pup may think it's something to play with.

> **TOO MUCH EXCITEMENT = NO ELIMINATION**
>
> Do not excite your dog when it's in the potty area. Overenthusiastic praise or too much chatter will cause a dog to tense its muscles and not finish the job. The dog will feel the urge to go again when it calms down, after you've taken it into the house. This situation is not the one that you want to encourage.

INTRODUCTION TO POTTY AREA

Let the dog out of its crate and take it on leash to its new toileting area. Indicate the spot you've scented with its urine. The familiar odor will give the dog a clue that this is the place to go. (If you are unable to scent a spot for your pup, just stand there and wait for it to make its own mark.)

Keep the dog leashed so it won't wander away. Stand quietly and let it sniff around in the designated area. If your pup starts to leave before it has eliminated, gently lead it back and remind it to go. If your pup sniffs at the scented spot, praise it calmly and just wait. If it produces, praise serenely, then give it time to sniff around a little more. It may not be finished, so give it time to go again before allowing it to play and explore its new home.

POTTY AREA RULES

Take your pup to its potty place frequently throughout the day. Each time you successfully anticipate elimination

About
Housetraining

and help your pup to the potty spot, you'll move a step closer to your goal. Stay aware of your puppy's needs. If you ignore the pup, it will make mistakes and you'll be cleaning up more messes. The dog's understanding of house rules will suffer if you don't guide it carefully during the first couple of weeks it's in your home.

Don't fret if your pup doesn't eliminate every time you take it to its toileting area. Just familiarize the dog with the approved place and give it sufficient opportunities to go there. Try not to let it make mistakes in the house. Praising your dog for potty success will house-train it quicker than scolding for accidents. Most dogs can be house-trained without punishment by anticipating their needs and helping them form good habits.

IMMUNIZATION CONCERNS

Young pups that have not finished their vaccination series are at risk if exposed to canine diseases. Public areas where many dogs are walked can be hazardous for incompletely immunized pups. Germs may lurk invisibly in the grass or on the pathways. Walk your unprotected pup only in less-used areas and keep it away from any dog feces you see.

Be sure to keep your pup current on all immunizations. Up-to-date immunizations, along with a good diet, plenty of water, exercise and rest are the surest ways to keep your pup in the peak of health.

Timing Is Everything

A pup under 3 months may need to urinate every hour and will move its bowels as many times a day as it eats. Once past 4 months, its potty trips will be less frequent.

Keep a chart of your new dog's potty behavior for the first three or four days. Jot down what time it eats, sleeps and eliminates. After several days a pattern will emerge that can help you determine your pup's body rhythm. Most dogs tend to eliminate at fairly regular intervals. Once you know your new dog's natural rhythms, you'll be able to anticipate its needs and schedule appropriate potty outings. Your dog will have more successes than failures, and that will speed house-training.

THE FIRST NIGHT

Most dogs, even young ones, will not soil their beds if they can avoid it. For this reason, a sleeping crate can be a tremendous help during housetraining. Being crated at night can help a dog develop the muscles that control elimination. It will also learn that you're alert to its needs both day and night.

Bedtime

Just before bedtime, take your dog to its potty area. Stand by and wait until it produces. You must not put your dog to bed for the night until it has eliminated. Be patient and calm. This is not the time to play or excite your dog. If it's too excited, a pup not only won't pee or poop, it probably won't want to sleep either.

Take your puppy out to the potty area frequently— although it may not eliminate every time, you are establishing a familiar routine.

After your dog has emptied out, put it to bed.

A good place to put your dog's sleeping crate is near your own bed. Dogs are pack animals, so they feel safer sleeping with others in a common area. In your bedroom, the pup will be near you and you'll be close enough to hear when it wakes during the night needing to eliminate.

Mid-Sleep Outing

Pups under 4 months often are not able to hold their urine all night. If your puppy has settled down to sleep but awakens and fusses a few hours later, it probably needs to go potty. For best housetraining progress, take your pup to its elimination area whenever it needs to go, even in the wee hours of the morning.

TIMES FOR ELIMINATION

When a puppy first awakens, when it pauses in play and after it eats or drinks, it will need to eliminate. Always take a puppy to its potty area at those times. Those are universal elimination times for all dogs, including mature adults.

Your pup may soil in the crate if you ignore its late night urgency. It's unfair to let this happen and it sends the wrong message about expectations for cleanliness. Resign yourself to this mid-sleep outing and just get up and take the pup to potty. Your pup will outgrow this need soon, so you won't have to do this forever. With time, your pup will learn that it can count on you and you'll wake happily each morning to a clean dog.

The Second Day—Establishing a Routine

This will be your first full day with your new dog, so start off by teaching it a command to eliminate. Immediately upon waking, take your pup to the potty area and calmly command it to eliminate. Say, "Go potty," or, "Do business," or, "Urinate"; it doesn't matter what command you choose, any word or short phrase will work. Just pick a command you can say in public without embarrassment. Use the command consistently each time you take your dog to potty. After it eliminates, reward with praise that includes the command word, as in "Good potty" or "Good do business." Soon your dog will associate that word with the act and will eliminate on command.

On day two, first things first. Out to the potty area before anything else.

After your pup empties out in the morning, give it breakfast. Let it eat and drink until it's satisfied, then take it to its toileting area again. After that, it shouldn't need to eliminate again right away, so you can allow it some free playtime. Keep an eye on the pup though, because when it pauses in play, it may need to go potty. Take it to the right spot, give the command and praise if it produces. A young pup will sometimes fall asleep in the middle of play. Don't wake it to go potty, but be sure you take the pup to its elimination area as soon as it does awake.

Food

Pups younger than 4 months need three or four meals a day and free access to fresh drinking water. Nutritional needs are high in puppies, but holding capacity is small, so they must eat frequent small meals. The digestive system is closely allied with the elimination system. Eating sets them both in motion. A pup will move its bowels about as many times a day as it eats, so frequent meals mean frequent elimination.

Water

3

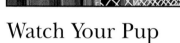

Make sure your dog has access to clean water at all times. Limiting the amount of water a dog drinks is not necessary for housetraining success and can be very dangerous.

Prevent accidents by limiting the dog's access—not by limiting its food and water.

Watch Your Pup

Never allow your pup out of your sight, either indoors or out, unless it's securely enclosed in its crate or puppy corral. When you're not able to watch your pup, it will make its own choices. If it's free to roam your house, you can bet it will choose inappropriate places to go potty. Be watchful. Help your pup avoid elimination accidents. Every potty mistake delays housetraining progress; every success speeds it along.

Vigilance now, during your new dog's first few weeks in your home, will pay big dividends. In the beginning you'll have to stay on full alert to keep your new pup out of trouble, but as time passes the pup will understand the rules better. Help your pup as much as you can right now; it's a stranger to your home and needs lots of guidance. Your job will become easier as the dog learns which behaviors earn praise.

> ## THE IMPORTANCE OF WATER
>
> Always allow your pup or adult dog access at all times to clean, fresh water. Limiting the amount of water a dog drinks is not necessary for housetraining and can cause serious illness or death.
>
> A dog needs water to digest food, maintain a proper temperature and proper blood volume and clean its system of toxins and wastes. A healthy dog will automatically drink the right amount. Do not restrict water intake.
>
> Controlling your dog's access to water is not the key to housetraining it, but controlling its access to everything else is.

Making

Housetraining

part two

Easy

Age-Appropriate

Housetraining

It really is amazing how fast a puppy grows and develops. The helpless infant turns into a chubby toddler at 5 weeks, a playful buddy at 6, a little explorer by 7 and is ready to conquer a new home at 8 weeks. Time flies, but it may sometimes seem that you've been mopping up after your puppy for ages. Don't worry, the situation will soon improve as each week brings your pup better control over its body.

Baby Puppy (4 to 7 weeks)

Puppies, like human babies, need time for their bodies and minds to develop before they can control their elimination. The younger your pup is, the longer before it will be able to be fully housetrained.

4 Weeks of Age

At 4 weeks old, a pup is much too young to grasp housetraining lessons. At that age, the pup should still be with its mama. It needs her company and body heat. A 4-week-old puppy still nurses and may not yet have tasted solid foods. Four weeks is too young to adopt a puppy unless it has no mother to care for it.

Age-Appropriate Housetraining

About the best housetraining tactic with a puppy this young is to train yourself. Spread plenty of newspaper on the floor of the pup's area. At 4 weeks, a pup will stay very close to its bed and food source. At first it will potty wherever it happens to be when nature calls. This is not a lack of cleanliness, it simply can't help it. At this age its eliminative functions are not yet voluntary. Bowel and bladder control develop gradually.

A very young puppy has no control over its elimination. You might want to simply spread out newspapers and wait until it develops some bladder and bowel control.

5 Weeks of Age

At about 5 weeks old, a pup usually begins eating a solid diet. The mother dog still may nurse her pups, but she no longer cleans up their wastes. Instead, after nursing, the dam leads her babies a short distance from the den to eliminate. A puppy with a good mother receives early potty training that way.

Five-week-old puppies really should stay with their mama for two more weeks. During that period, the mother dog will finish weaning her pups and will teach them doggie social graces like eliminating far away from the eating area. If you are housetraining a 5-week-old pup, you'll have to take it to the potty place many times a day. This is time-consuming and isn't practical for many owners. Some people opt to just spread papers over the entire puppy corral floor and wait a few weeks before beginning serious housetraining.

6 WEEKS OF AGE

When it reaches 6 weeks of age, a pup can adjust to a new home, although it is still quite young to leave its littermates. It's also a bit early to expect much bladder and bowel control. You can, however, begin housetraining a puppy this age, but the "training" will really consist of you learning to take the infant to the potty spot before it wets or messes.

At 6 weeks, a pup may need hourly opportunities to visit the potty spot or it may need to go less frequently. Get to know your pup's body rhythms by charting pees and poops for several days. That will give you a rough idea of your pup's elimination timing and help you anticipate its needs.

7 WEEKS OF AGE

By about 7 weeks of age, a pup will feel the urge to eliminate coming on, then try to get away from food and bedding areas to do its job. This signals readiness to begin housetraining. The puppy will still need to eliminate every hour or two, but with encouragement it can begin to understand that there is an approved place for potty.

When your pup is depositing most of its messes toward the far end of its corral, you can begin to shift the papered area to that end. Widen the gap between the bedding and the potty papers by only a few inches each day. Gradual change will work best at this stage. Don't uncover too many inches of floor between the bed and potty areas or your puppy may not know what it is supposed to do. If the pup thinks the potty papers have disappeared entirely, it will do its business on the uncovered floor. Make it easy for your pup to understand.

At about 7 weeks, your pup can start learning a word for elimination. Having an actual command for this is

THE BEST AGE TO BUY A PUP

Only in cases of dire necessity should a puppy be taken from its dam before 6 weeks of age. Most experienced breeders and behavior specialists agree that the period between 7 and 9 weeks is the right time for a puppy to go to its permanent home. At that age, the pup is learning social behavior and is ready to start bonding with a human family. That is a good time to make the transfer from the mama and sibling-pack to the new family-pack of people and, maybe, other pets.

extremely handy. You'll be able to take your pup to the spot you select, say the command and the pup will do its business right away. A potty command will make it easier for you to control where and when your dog does its business.

Developing Control

As a pup matures, bowel control develops first, then bladder control. At 7 weeks of age, most pups have begun to gain some control over elimination, but don't expect any housetraining miracles yet. The pup may still just squat to piddle wherever it happens to be when the urge arrives, then go back to play as if nothing had happened. This is natural, so you had best be vigilant whenever your puppy is freed from its enclosure.

Young Puppy (8 to 15 weeks)

An 8-week-old pup needs a chance to potty about every two hours. It may need to go more often if it's been playing vigorously and drinking water to cool off. Keep in mind the four key times a pup needs to eliminate: after waking, eating, drinking or playing. Take your puppy to the elimination spot at those times and any other time the pup seems to need it.

Eight-week-old pups get enough warning before eliminating that they will try to get away from their bed and food before emptying out. At about this age, you can begin decreasing the size of the papered area in the pup's playpen. Put potty papers at the opposite side of the corral from the pup's resting and eating area. It's best if the papers are located at the end of the pen closest to the door leading outside. The pup will get accustomed to walking toward that door when it has to go potty, which will set a pattern that facilitates housetraining.

If you just leave the pup by itself in its corral all day, it will have no choice but to potty there. This will not put you closer to your goals. Pups develop habits very rapidly, and you want to make sure that the habits your puppy develops are good ones. The more times each day your pup eliminates in the approved area, the faster good habits will be formed.

Each time you take your puppy to the potty spot, quietly command it to eliminate. Praise softly after it's finished. Soon your pup will recognize the elimination command and will do its business when and where you say.

THE POTTY BELL

Introduce your pup to ringing a bell when it needs to go potty. Hang a bell or string of bells from the handle of the door that leads to the potty place. The bell should hang at puppy nose level. Be sure the bell is sufficiently loud to be heard from the next room. You won't always see your pup ring, but you'll hear the sound of the bell.

Your pup will display body signals when it feels the urge to eliminate. The pup may sniff around anxiously, circle, head down the hall, or give some other clue that it's getting ready to potty. When your puppy looks like it may need to relieve itself, say, "Let's go potty outside." Ring the bell before you open the door, then escort the pup out to its approved spot.

THE "SHADOW" LEASH

Leash your puppy to your belt when it's out of its corral. Make it your little shadow, so even if your attention is not directed solely at your pup, it will not be able to wander off to potty in an unapproved spot. You will notice when your pup seems restless when it needs to eliminate, and you'll be right there to take it to the potty place and praise it if it goes.

When you see your pup sniffling and circling, take it out to its potty spot.

Don't worry about specifically training the pup to ring the bell. It will see you do it each time you take it out to potty. The way a dog thinks, whatever precedes an event is the cause of the event. So, if you ring the bell before opening the door, your pup will get the idea that ringing the bell causes the door to open. When it makes this connection it will try ringing the bell so the door will open. When you hear the bell, hurry to the door to take your pup outside. Praise it for letting you know it has to go.

If you brought your pup home at 7 or 8 weeks of age, by 10 weeks it may already have learned to ring the potty bell when it needs to go out. It's probably also aware that there's a certain place to go potty. The pup may have no idea how to get to that special spot without your help, though, so you should continue to escort your puppy to its potty area. That is the only way you can be sure it will form the good habits you want it to have, and you'll be right there to praise for doing duty in the correct place.

Previous Home Environment

If you adopt a pup 12 to 15 weeks old that has been kept in a clean environment and educated by its mama about clean potty habits, you should have little trouble housetraining it. At this stage, a pup gets enough advance warning when it has to eliminate that it has time to ask to go out. It will not always have perfect timing yet, so be patient and understanding. Continue to praise for potty in the right place and be sure to praise when the pup lets you know it needs to go.

If you adopt a pup at 12 to 15 weeks that has been kept in unsanitary quarters, you'll have to work hard to teach it clean habits. Be patient, consistent and compassionate. Give the pup time and you'll succeed in housetraining it.

A new pup from a deprived or dirty environmental background will need a lot of attention. You must stay vigilant with this pup. Watch for its potty signals as carefully as you would with a very young puppy. You'll learn your pup's potty signals and catch it in time if you are on your toes.

Although the pup from a dirty kennel may be physically normal, it may not try to move away from its bed and food before eliminating. This pup is not used to having any part of its environment free of waste. It may take longer than average for this pup to learn clean habits. On the other hand, the puppy may be so happy to have a decent-smelling place to sleep and eat that it catches on quickly.

A crate is good place for a dog to rest and relax, but it is cruel to leave a young dog crated all day long.

CRATE OR CORRAL

A pup can hold its urine for only about as many hours as its age in months. A 2-month-old pup will pee about every two hours, while at 4 months it can manage about four hours between piddles. Pups vary somewhat in their rate of development, so this is not a hard and fast rule. It does, however, present a realistic idea of how long a pup can be left without access to a potty place.

**APPROPRIATE
CONFINEMENT**

A crate may be used to confine a puppy for one or two hours, but an indoor or outdoor pen should be used if it must be left unattended for longer periods. Confine the puppy in a safe puppy corral with room to play and papers for elimination. The pup will be able to maintain its healthy, natural body rhythms without using the rest of your home as its toilet. If it has opportunity to eliminate only in approved areas, the pup won't be confused about where to go and will become housetrained sooner.

Older Puppy (4 to 6 months)

By 16 weeks of age, most puppies have fairly good bladder and bowel control. They now have enough advance warning to ask to go to the designated potty area and enough time to get there. By 4 to 6 months of age, a pup raised with a potty bell will be ringing it to notify owners when it needs to go out. The pup may not be fully housetrained at this age, but it's getting close.

If you adopt a pup this age, hopefully it has already had introductory housetraining. If the pup has been raised and kept in a clean environment with access to a toileting area, the pup may already have the right idea. It might even be almost fully housetrained.

On the other hand, if you adopt a pup this age that has always had to live in its own filth, you should proceed with housetraining as if the dog was a very young pup. It will be able to hold its elimination for longer periods, but it has no more accurate idea of the proper place to go than a young baby pup does. Be very patient and vigilant.

Adolescent Dog (7 to 12 months)

At 7 months, a pup has nearly reached its full growth and is close to attaining adult bladder and bowel control. With this maturity may come the desire to mark territory. Adolescent and adult male dogs are especially likely to mark, but many females also do.

Urine and feces carry a dog's unique body scent. Dogs urinate, and may defecate, to mark the borders of their turf and at regular checkpoints along their daily walking route. Some dogs also scuff the ground with their hind feet, scratching the surface soil, after they have eliminated. A dog has scent-producing glands on its footpads, so scuffing leaves odor and a visual mark as well.

An adolescent dog's instinct is to mark everything it can. When out walking your dog, train it to urinate on command— constant marking is a nuisance!

MARKING

Some adult male dogs, if al-lowed to mark as often as they like, may take two hours to walk around one block. Don't misunderstand your adolescent dog's urge to urinate so frequently. The dog isn't peeing so often because it can't hold its bladder, it's actually rationing each squirt so that it doesn't run out before it gets home. If it was only urinating for comfort, it could get the job done with just one stop. You will not create a hardship for your dog if you don't let it pee on every pillar and post.

When you walk an adolescent dog, it's a good tactic to curb its desire to mark repeatedly along the route— marking is about turf. A dog claims all the real estate it can by wetting it with urine. If allowed to do this at will, your dog may mark more and more frequently until it's stopping at every bush and blade of grass. Prevent this natural impulse behavior from getting out of control by allowing your dog to urinate on walks only when you stop and tell it to.

Adult Dog (1 to 7 years)

A healthy adult dog can control its eliminative functions about as well as adult humans. During adulthood, there are seldom any problems with elimination control, except during illness or trauma. Medical and environmental conditions may affect elimination in an adult dog. If a problem suddenly crops up, you should take the dog to the veterinarian for a physical checkup.

Moving to a New House

One common nonmedical cause for an adult dog to break housetraining is a move to a new home. Until a dog can adjust to the new surroundings, there may be a few potty problems. As a dog settles in to its new territory, it will probably leave urine to register its claim on the new turf. By establishing a border of scent posts, the dog warns other animals that the area is occupied.

Some dogs, while marking their boundaries to prove ownership of a new property, may also decide to mark items inside the house. If this occurs, take the dog to the newly marked spot, indicate what it's done and give it a short scolding. Then take the dog outside to a spot that is permissible to mark and command it to eliminate. Praise the dog for marking the permitted spot.

You should watch the dog very carefully for a few weeks as it becomes accustomed to the new place to prevent it from marking the wrong spots.

Senior Dog (7 years and older)

In its senior years, a dog's body gradually starts to wear down. Sometimes certain systems suddenly deteriorate. Older dogs may begin to have less control of their eliminative functions, and they occasionally become incontinent for one or more reasons. Illness or hormone imbalance may cause an older dog to break housetraining. Sometimes muscles lose their hold during sleep or exercise and some urine or feces leaks out. Whatever the cause, age-related incontinence is not intentional and cannot be trained away; it is a physical disability that must be humanely managed. If your senior aged dog begins to have trouble with its elimination, be compassionate and try to help as much as possible.

Some older dogs may develop problems with their housetraining skills. If this occurs, have your dog examined by a veterinarian. There are many reasons behind incontinence in older dogs.

A dog must never be punished for soiling when it cannot control itself, not as a little puppy and certainly not in old age. Shaming an old dog for an unintentional breach of housetraining is insensitive and cruel. An owner might be very upset to wake up or arrive home to a mess, but it's not the old dog's fault. The dog needs emotional support for this loss of dignity, not a scolding.

If you notice your mature dog seems to have less control of its elimination than usual, take it to the veterinarian right away. The dog could be developing old-age incontinence, but it could have a different problem that is unrelated to its age. In all likelihood, with help from your veterinarian, you'll be able to make your dog comfortable and happy through its senior years.

chapter 5

Paper- Training

Advantages and Disadvantages of Paper-Training

Many owners start a young pup's potty training indoors on newspapers or puddle pads. A papered surface may already be familiar to the pup from its former home. There is a choice of paper products that can be used to cover the floor in a pup's elimination area.

NEWSPAPER

Newspaper is abundant, absorbent and inexpensive—a great combination for the purpose at hand. Newspaper sections can be opened and overlapped to cover a large surface of floor. They can soak up quite a large puddle and are easy to pick up after use. Stacks of newspaper accumulate quickly when people read one or more daily. If your own reserves run low, put out the call to a few friends. Ask them to check their back porches and garages for newspaper. This might be just the excuse your friends have been waiting for to come meet your adorable puppy. Before long, you'll have a plentiful supply of newspaper and some new friends for your pup.

Although smudgy, newspaper is actually clean—nearly sterile from the heat involved in the printing process. The old toxic, metal-based inks used years ago to print newspapers have been replaced now by vegetable-based pigments. These new inks are still a bit messy and will smudge your hands as you spread them, but they are no longer toxic. The small amounts of soy ink that rub off newspapers onto a pup's feet should be safe. If you are concerned about toxicity of a news-paper's ink, call the paper's print shop. Find out what type of ink they use and then ask your veterinarian if it's safe for puppies.

The main disadvantage to using newspaper to house-train a pup is its smudginess. This is only a very minor problem as the ink easily washes off with soap and water. News ink can be messy on light-colored fur but, again, this can be washed away. If you prefer to avoid the ink problem but still wish to paper-train your pup, there are a few commercial alternatives.

It may be possible to purchase a huge roll of unprinted newspaper from your local newspaper, or from a paper supply wholesaler. This paper has no ink on it, so it creates no smudges. The rolled paper is lacking one advantage of the printed and folded product: It must be torn off in big pieces and numerous layers spread. The folded sections are convenient because they're several pages thick.

A rather humorous drawback to housetraining a pup on newspaper is that a dog trained to use the surface for potty will seek it out for that purpose. This becomes a problem only if someone drops the Sunday news on the floor and leaves the room. More than one puppy owner has returned to find the financial section flooded.

Puddle Pads

A convenient, though more expensive, alternative to newspaper is a commercial puppy puddle pad. These are sold under several trade names. The pads are similar to disposable diapers and are made of absorbent layers of paper, backed by a waterproof sheet of plastic. Some puddle pads are scented with an odor that is designed to "call" a pup there to eliminate. Other brands have perfumes to make them pleasing to the human nose.

Puddle pads are usually about half the size of a sheet of newspaper, which means that you'll need to spread several, overlapping them at the edges, to create a large enough target for your pup to hit. For this reason, puddle pads are most suitable for small pups and toy breeds.

Where to Put the "Indoor Toilet"

The average pup will not be reliably housetrained before 16 weeks of age. There will be steady progress along the way if you follow this book's advice, but it will take time for a pup's body systems to mature. Even after pups have mastered approved potty behavior, most must still be confined when left alone to prevent trash raiding, furniture sitting, kitty stalking and other doggie misdemeanors.

Your pup's indoor corral will be in use for several months, so it should be in a convenient central location. You have probably heard the adage: "No matter where I serve my guests, they seem to like my kitchen best." People tend to congregate in the kitchen, which provides company and positive social experience for a pup. In the kitchen, your pup will have company, receive attention and training and feel like a member of the family. Moreover, a kitchen typically has a washable floor and often a door leading to a potential outdoor potty area.

Some owners use a bathroom, laundry room, mud room or porch for their pup's area. If this room is connected to the kitchen and is a high traffic area, it may be quite suitable. However, if the room that you choose is in a quiet corner of the house, this site may not be very good for your pup. A pup tucked out of the mainstream will receive less attention from people. This will slow its education and hold it back socially. An isolated pup won't see its owners as often as it should, won't get to play interactive games, won't be learning commands and won't be a very happy camper. Why bring a puppy home if you plan to ignore it?

Isolated pups can not reach their highest potential for intelligence. They need mental stimulation to grow. Puppies need almost constant socialization to become attentive, obedient and without fear or aggression. Lonely pups dig up the flooring and try to jump the gate for exercise. They bark and whine and dine on walls for entertainment. If your puppy is tucked away by itself, it cannot form the high-quality bond with you that is the greatest joy of owning a dog.

Setting Up Your Pup's Playpen

Imagine, for a moment, that your pup's playpen is a wild dog's cave in the wilderness. The wild dog's bed would be at the back of its den for security. Near the sleeping spot is a pile of bones from the dog's recent meal. The den's opening leads to the place where the wild dog eliminates. It keeps its bed and den clean, but likes to mark with urine just outside, letting rivals know on whose territory they are trespassing.

Place your pup's bed or crate and its bowls and toys at the end of its playpen farthest from the door or gate. When the puppy moves away from its bed to go potty, it will also be moving toward the door that leads to an approved outdoor potty area. This forms a good habit and helps when introducing outdoor potty training.

When you first bring your pup home, the whole floor of the indoor playpen should be covered wall to wall with newspaper or puddle pads. The pup will get used to going potty on the paper and learn to seek that texture underfoot when it needs to eliminate. Paper-training is often the most convenient way to teach young pups that there are approved places to go potty, which helps the pup understand that there are also for-

bidden spots. Even little puppies can understand that only part of the world is covered with potty paper.

A very young pup will barely step away from its bed before eliminating. As its body matures the puppy will walk farther away from its sleeping nest to go potty. When you notice that your pup is pooping and peeing a few feet from its bed, begin shrinking the potty paper area.

Start by leaving a narrow strip of bare floor between the pup's bed and the papers. This gap should be no wider than the pup's body length. It's important the pup

Begin shrinking the area covered with paper as you find the puppy moving away from its bed to eliminate.

understands it is still to use the papers, but must cross bare floor to get to them. If the gap is too wide, the puppy may miss the target and pee on the uncovered floor. This is not what you want. Success reinforces clean behavior. If you give your puppy every opportunity to be clean, it will learn quicker and cooperate better with housetraining.

SAFETY

The puppy space should be disaster-proofed before you leave your new furry friend alone for even a moment. Get down on your hands and knees to the pup's eye level. Take a good look around. You'll see the whole world, or at least your kitchen, from a very different view down at puppy height. Be sure that whatever you see will not be dangerous to, or ruined by, your curious puppy.

Check all floor-level cabinets to be certain that latches can't be opened by puppy paws or teeth. Put all electrical cords out of chewing range. Doors to the room must be closed securely or gated to prevent escape. Gates should lock securely into place, yet be easily opened with one hand. Easy-open gates for doorways can be purchased at department, pet and children's stores.

ALTERNATE INDOOR OPTION— THE LITTER BOX

Some owners prefer their dogs to use a litter box instead of papers as an indoor potty place. Using a litter box is really only feasible with small breeds. A litter box is easy to take along when traveling or RV camping. A disadvantage is the messy litter that the dog may track out of the box. Litter-box training for dogs is not common, but it can be a very workable solution for a little dog's potty needs.

Make sure that the gate you choose really is escape-proof!

The Box

Be sure you get a litter box that's wide enough for your dog to turn around in and at least 6 inches longer than the dog's body. The box should be about 6 inches deep. Most litter pans designed for cats are not large enough for any but the smallest dogs. A better box might be the large, shallow, plastic type made to slide under a bed for blanket storage. These come in several sizes, all bigger than most pet litter pans. Save the lid that comes with the storage box. If, in the future, you decide to teach your dog to ask to use its box, you can train it to scratch the lid as a signal. (The lid is also very handy to keep the contents of the box intact if you are traveling.)

The Litter

There are different types of litter that you can use in a potty box. The simplest is to line it with newspaper or a puddle pad. Some people tear or shred newspaper to use as litter. Kitty litter can be used, but more may end

51

up on the floor than you'd like. Unlike cats, dogs do not cover their messes. Some dogs do scuff and scrape behind them with their rear feet after they've pooped. This tosses dirt around so as to leave visual signs for other dogs. Not every dog does this, but one that has this habit will send kitty litter flying all over the place. A better choice than loose litter might be pelletized newspaper or wood dust. The pieces are larger and not as messy as kitty litter.

SWITCHING FROM PAPERS TO LITTER BOX

To switch from papers to a litter box, follow the same steps as if switching to outdoors. Take a section of newspaper or a puddle pad with a bit of the dog's urine and place this in the empty litter box. Put the box in the pup's corral where the potty paper area was. When potty time rolls around, place your puppy in the litter box to stand on the same familiar paper that has been its elimination surface on the floor. The idea of the litter box is brand-new to your pup, and it may think it odd. If the pup seems confused or worried, tell it what a good pup it is. Praise it if it stays in the box. Praise it again if it sniffs the paper. If it eliminates, quietly tell it what a wonderful dog it is for being so quick and cooperative about this new lesson.

If the puppy hops out of the box, calmly lift it back in and tell it to go potty. If it sniffs at the papers, praise it. If it jumps out again, gently help it back in. Be calm and gentle about this or you'll scare the pup and it may never want to use a litter box. If the pup hops out of the box and pees on the papered floor, don't worry and don't scold or shame the pup. You will have other chances to teach use of the litter box, in fact, one about every two hours.

The calmer and more matter-of-fact you are, the sooner your pup will accept the litter box. Be patient and persistent; you will win.

TRANSITION TO OUTDOORS

It is not difficult to switch a pup from indoor papertraining to outdoor elimination. Owners of large pups often switch early, but potty papers are still useful if the pup spends time in its indoor corral while you're away. Remember, a pup 3 months old needs to potty at least every three hours; a 4-month-old every four hours; 5 months, five hours and so on. Use the papers as long as your pup needs them. If you come home and they haven't been soiled, you are ahead.

Most owners use a combination of indoor papers and outdoor elimination areas. When the pup is left by itself in the playpen, it can potty on the ever-present newspaper. When you are available to take the pup outside, it can do its business in the outdoor spot. This works well for many owners, and no big transition is necessary when the pup makes the final switch over to outdoor potty.

To help a pup adapt to the change from indoors to outdoors, take one of its potty papers outside to the new elimination area. Let the pup stand on the paper when it goes potty outdoors. Each day for four days, reduce the size of the paper by half. By the fifth day, the pup, having used a smaller and smaller piece of paper to stand on, will probably just go to that spot and eliminate.

Eventually, the pup will need no visual clue to take care of business outdoors.

PRE-SCENTING THE POTTY SPOT

A soiled sheet of newspaper or a used puddle pad carries the scent of the pup's waste. Put that down in the outdoor toileting area. Place a small rock on the paper to prevent a breeze from taking it away.

When it's potty time, leash your pup, take it to the marked outdoor spot and give the command you use for potty. If the pup sniffs the paper, praise it gently and encourage it to do its business. If it starts to wander away, quietly lead it back to the paper and command it again to go potty.

53

SHRINKING THE VISUAL TARGET

When your pup has made the connection between potty on paper inside and potty on paper outside, shrink the target area. Leave just a 6-inch piece of paper weighted with a stone. The paper won't be large enough to stand on, so your dog will have to potty on the ground. Be sure to praise it warmly, but not excitedly, when it does. (Excited praise may cause a dog to tense up and not be able to finish eliminating.)

The final step in the transition to outdoor potty is to remove the visual clue (the paper) and replace it with scent only. Do this by taking a paper with the pup's urine on it and pouring water through it onto the ground below. The water will carry the urine scent and mark the spot for your pup.

It is fairly easy, but time-intensive, to teach a pup to potty in one designated area only. To train your dog to do this, always take it to the same spot at potty time. Don't let it dawdle along the way or it might pee somewhere else instead. Always take the pup to visit the official potty spot before leaving the yard with it for walks. The dog shouldn't get its walk until it has produced in the potty area. This means you won't have to worry so much about picking up poops on exercise walks. Your dog will already have done its business at home.

Be patient. Housetraining is as big a challenge for your dog as it is for you.

SURFACE PROBLEM

A pup's potty behavior is connected to its tactile memory of the footing in the elimination area. A problem may occur if your dog came from a home where it was used to eliminating on grass but you happen to be a city dweller with only a paved terrace or patio to offer.

The solution isn't as hard as some would imagine. Just call a landscape company and buy a short roll of sod grass. Put the grass on your patio and teach your dog to eliminate there. Over a period of a week or two, decrease the size of the sod until your dog is eliminating on the paved surface.

Outdoor

Training

Some dogs go potty just about any-where they want and, as long as they don't soil in the house, the owners are pleased. Few people realize they could refine their dog's habits. You can actually be quite specific about where you allow your dog to eliminate. While you are teaching the pup to go potty outside, have it confine its elimination to one particular area.

Selecting an Appropriate Elimination Place

The majority of dog owners train their dogs to eliminate outside, even if they start them indoors on newspaper. For some dogs, outdoor potty means acres to roam, for some it's a grassy yard or a concrete run, still for others it's a leash walk to the curb. Whatever your living situation, selecting a suitable location for your dog's outdoor potty area will speed housetraining.

People with large yards leave a patch at the edge of the lawn unmowed to serve as the dog's elimination area. Other dog owners teach the dog to relieve in a designated corner of a deck or patio. For an apartment-dwelling city dog, the outdoor potty area might be a tiny balcony or the curb between parked cars. Each dog owner has somewhat different expectations for their dog. Teach your dog to eliminate in a spot that suits your environment and lifestyle.

An ideal outdoor potty area would be flat or gently sloping and less than 50 feet from your door. The path leading to it should have no deep mud or prickly weeds to walk through and should be lighted for safe use at night. Places that fit this profile may be anywhere from a garden to a gutter. If you have a choice of where to have your dog eliminate, remember that the easier you make it for your dog to eliminate in the right place, the sooner it will be housetrained.

POTTY SPOT CRITERIA

The outdoor area you select for your dog's elimination spot should meet three important criteria. It should be:

- close

- convenient, and

- cleanable.

A nearby spot helps ensure that your dog will get to it in time. A convenient spot will make it more likely that you will accompany your dog—you get to praise it for doing the right thing! The benefits of a spot that is easy to clean are obvious—less work for you and a more pleasant experience for your dog. Remember, your dog wants a clean area to go to. It will ultimately reject a spot that is dirty.

Country Dogs

A rural home is great for dogs. They love to romp through forests and fields, wade streams and explore trails. Out in the country, one might feel as if we could step back in time to when dogs could safely run free. Times really have changed, though, and roaming free is dangerous for dogs and also illegal in many locales. In the country, loose dogs risk injury from vehicles, animals, poisons, stray bullets and other adventure-related hazards. Your dog will be safer and probably live years longer if you keep it home. Neighbors may be happier and friendlier, too, if you keep your dog on your property.

If you can keep an impressionable young pup from wandering off, it will form the good habit of staying home. On the other hand, if you just turn your pup loose without guidance, it will find plenty of trouble to get into and may develop the dangerous habit of wandering. Do whatever you must do to keep your pup from starting the roaming habit. Once a dog becomes a vagabond, even a huge acreage will not be enough to keep it home.

Safe Confinement

To keep your dog safe and at home, unless you can watch it every moment, you'll need to confine it somehow. Whether you live in town or out in the boondocks, a well-fenced backyard is the best solution for keeping a dog happy, healthy and home.

Chains, ropes, and cable tie-outs are inexpensive but dangerous because

A fenced yard is undoubtedly the best environment that you can provide for your dog. An urban pet may enjoy access to a patio, so long as it is well enclosed.

they can tangle and sometimes strangle dogs. Freestanding chain-link wire kennel runs are convenient to install, but are lonely, cramped and uncomfortable for a dog. A kennel run can work as a dog's potty place, but it has quite a few drawbacks compared to a fenced yard. You must take your dog from the house out to its kennel each time it has to eliminate. If it's more than a few steps from the door, you may soon find yourself tempted to leave it in the kennel too long.

A FENCED YARD IS BEST

A fenced yard allows convenient access to and from the house and does not isolate the dog from the rest of the family.

Outdoor potty training will be easiest for both you and your dog if your yard can be fenced to include one of the doors to your home. That will allow you to let the pup in and out without having to dress for the weather.

With a fenced yard, you can easily go with your dog to the potty place while you're housetraining it. After the dog is trained, you might consider letting it use a pet door to let itself in and out at will.

Suburban Dogs

Small towns and suburbs have many homes with yards. Suburban householders often go to considerable effort and expense to beautify their property. Their understandable pride in home and yard sometimes presents a problem when a dog joins the family. Where can a dog's potty area be located that won't sully the view and spoil the landscaping?

Suburban yards are often bordered by hedges or other plantings. This is a nice way to mark the edges of the property, adding beauty as well as privacy. A fenced area for the new dog can be disguised with decorative plantings. A fence, hidden by attractive foliage, makes a property more secure without giving the appearance of a fortress.

THE JOYS OF A FENCED YARD

To keep your dog safe, and at home, you'll need to confine it somehow. Regardless of where you live, a well-fenced backyard is the best solution for keeping a dog happy, healthy and home. A fenced yard allows convenient access to and from the house. Not only will you protect your dog, but you will not isolate it from its human family. A good people connection is important to a dog because it makes it feel it's part of the pack and subject to pack rules.

City Dogs

Housetraining your pup or dog in the city will differ depending upon the neighborhood you live in. If you are a fortunate city dweller, you may have access to a dogs-allowed courtyard or park where you could exercise and potty your pup. Otherwise, outdoor potty in the big city means your dog must be trained to eliminate at the curb.

In the city, you must pick up after your pooch whenever it defecates. Not only do you owe that courtesy to your neighbors, cleaning up after your dog benefits dogs and dog owners everywhere. Parks that allow dogs off-leash are becoming scarce, due largely to problems with unmannerly dog owners. Piles of poop dotting walkways and playgrounds are a major cause of cities closing their parks to dogs. The best way to counter this is to get rid of the evidence. Pick up your dog's poop. Every time! Even when nobody's watching, even at night, even when the weather is horrible. If every dog owner picked up every time, public parks would be cleaner, and more of them would probably be open to dogs.

DOG PARKS

Some city dog owners have convinced local powers to open specified areas of public parks for off-leash dog play and training. Off-leash dog parks are gradually appearing in cities around the nation. Some dog parks are private, with membership dues and identification cards, while others are open to the public. Most, but not all, dog parks are fenced to keep dogs safe from traffic and from running off. Dogs play and run and romp while owners watch and chat. When dogs stop playing to do their business, owners stop chatting to do cleanup duty. Some dog parks are equipped with plastic bag dispensers or poop scoops, making it easier for owners to comply with pick up rules.

Whether you're in a dog park or your own yard, clean up after your dog!

Training for Outdoor Elimination

To train your dog to eliminate outdoors, leash it and take it out to the area you've selected as its potty place. Mark the spot with a scent of the dog's own urine to help make training easier.

MANAGING DISTRACTIONS

The outside world is a very busy place, and at first your dog may be distracted by all that's around it. Each time the pup is about to eliminate, something new may catch its attention and cause it to hold back. This can make the first few outside potty attempts frustrating for new owners. Be patient, the situation will improve. In a few days, your pup will get used to typical outdoor distractions and will be able to concentrate on business.

Do not allow your pup to wander away from the potty area before it produces. If it tries to leave, gently lead it back and calmly repeat the command to potty. If your pup will not go, it could be that it doesn't need to yet. If you are keeping track of your dog's average daily elimination schedule, you'll know whether this is likely to be the problem. If the dog would normally go potty at this time, just be patient. Nature is on your side. The pup can't hold it forever.

Another reason your dog might not potty is that it's too excited to relax the muscles that control elimination. You can solve this problem by waiting calmly and occasionally reminding the dog to do its business. Stay in one place; don't let your pup lead you around, looking for the "perfect" spot. You have already shown the dog where to go, now just wait quietly. Your pup will go if it needs to.

WHEN THE PUP WON'T ELIMINATE

If you find yourself waiting more than five minutes for your dog to potty, take it back inside. Watch your pup carefully for twenty minutes, not giving it any opportunity to slip away to potty unnoticed. If you are too busy to watch the pup, put it in its crate. After twenty minutes, take it to the outdoor potty spot again and tell it what to do. If unsuccessful after five minutes, crate the dog again. Give it another chance to eliminate in fifteen or twenty minutes. Eventually, it will have to go. Be vigilant, don't let the pup make a mistake in the house. Training will progress much faster if you praise your pup rather than if you scold it.

COPING WITH ACCIDENTS

When your pup does have potty accidents, do not punish! It's not the pup's fault, it's yours for not watching closely enough. Take your pup and a paper towel to the mess. Point to the urine or feces and calmly tell your puppy, "No potty here." Then scoop or sop up the accident with the paper towel. Take the evidence and the pup to the approved potty area. Smear the pee or drop the mess on the ground (throw away the paper towel) and tell the dog, "Good potty here," as if it had done the deed there in the right place. Soon the puppy will understand that there is a place where you are pleased about potty and other places where you are not. Praising for elimination in the approved place will help your pup remember the rules.

When accidents happen, don't reprimand your dog. Praising for elimination in the approved place is far more effective.

DOG DOORS

A special door for your dog, opening out to a safely fenced yard, can be a real boon for dogs that must spend long hours alone. Pet doors can be installed in any door or wall and several styles are available. Most consist of a rigid frame holding a flexible flap that swings open when the dog pushes with its nose. Some models have a rigid door that's hinged to the frame along one side, like a regular door. Another type of pet door is a panel that fits into the opening of a sliding glass door. Pet doors come in a variety of sizes to fit any companion animal from a kitty to a Great Dane.

Crate-Training

Its hunger satisfied, the wild wolf relaxes in its den after feasting on game from the hunt. It lounges in its den opening, under the boughs of a fallen tree, where the earth is soft and easy to dig. The wolf built its den big enough to turn around and lie down in, yet small enough that its own heat can warm the space. Here the wolf can retreat from danger and rest safely. The den is a private place, a place of security. No wolf would be happy without its den.

Most modern dogs, at first glance, bear little resemblance to their wolf ancestors. Some of their behavior, however, is quite like that of their wild kin. One similarity is the canine preference for lounging in cavelike dens. It's not unusual for a pet dog to retreat under a table or chair when it chews on a bone. This is the closest thing to a cave available to many modern dogs.

Crate-Dens

There is a nice cave substitute you can provide for your dog that in some ways is even better than a real den because it's portable, clean and comfortable. This modern cave is called a travel crate or sleeping kennel. Not only will it give your dog a private sleeping and lounging area, the crate can be a great help with housetraining.

You may have seen crate-dens in your friends' homes or in pet supply stores. The two main types are folding wire or rigid plastic. The plastic crates have ventilation holes along both sides and a metal- or plastic-grated door. The top and bottom sections of the molded plastic crates come apart and nest together for storage. The wire type of crate is made of sturdy welded wire panels, hinged together to fold flat for storage. There are other styles, but these are the models most often used for housetraining.

Plastic Crates

Inside the plastic kennel, both light and sound are subdued, making it a soothing environment for the dog to spend time alone. These crates don't rattle or squeak when the dog moves around, so they are not a noisy annoyance while you are trying to sleep. The plastic kennels are sturdy, secure, easy to clean and many are airline-approved for travel safety.

Wire Crates

Wire crates are easy to set up and fold flat for easy storage, but are not safety-approved for air travel. They are open to air and light on the top and all sides. If a room is warm, this allows for better air circulation, but when the air is cool, a wire crate can be drafty. The wire panels tend to rattle when the dog moves around, which can be annoying to both you and the dog. A wire crate can be made quieter and less drafty by covering the top and sides with a blanket. A cover also makes the space more private, which most dogs like.

If your pup has a potty accident in a wire crate, although the watertight pan keeps wetness from seeping out the bottom, the mess may spill out the sides. Cleanup of a wire crate requires scrubbing each wire and welded junction individually and is more work than cleaning the same mess from a plastic crate. Although both types of crates have their strong points, all in all, the plastic crate is often the best choice for housetraining.

Introducing the Crate

It may take a little while to get used to the crate, but most dogs like the cozy space once they are accustomed to it. When first placed in a crate, a dog doesn't know if it will ever get out again. That causes some dogs to be anxious until they realize the crate is both comfortable and temporary. After spending a few short periods in the crate, the dog will learn that you'll always come back and let it out. Most dogs like the crate and go into it voluntarily when they want a private place.

To help introduce your dog to its crate, tie the door open and let the pup explore it on its own.

If your dog has not yet learned about crates, you should introduce it in as pleasant a manner as possible. Tie the door open and put the crate where the pup can explore it. Toss in a few treats or toys and encourage the dog to go in and get them. Some are afraid to go in at first, while others dash in without hesitation.

Whichever approach your pup takes, be patient. The introduction will be more successful if it isn't forced.

After your pup has gone in and out of the crate a few times and isn't worried about it any more, send it in after a treat and quietly shut the door for just a moment. Praise the pup, then open the door, give it another treat and let it out. Praise it for coming out, too. Make a game of going in and out. Send the pup in, close the door, praise it, let it out, praise it again. Wait a few seconds longer each time before letting the pup out.

LEAVE THE ROOM

When your pup can stay calmly in the crate for five minutes with you present, it's time for the next step. Put your dog in its crate with something safe and yummy to chew, then go into the next room and wait for one minute. Return to your pup and praise it calmly. If it seems happy chewing on its bone or toy, leave for fifteen minutes, then return and let it out.

It is possible that instead of enjoying its chewie, your pup puts up a terrible fuss about being left alone. If this is the case, stay out of sight for one minute, then go back to your pup as if nothing was out of the ordinary.

Do not scold and do not apologize. Just tell the pup quietly that it's a good dog, then leave the room again. If it starts to fuss again, go back to it quickly, slap your hand on the top of the crate and say sharply, "Hush!" This will startle your pup and should stop the noise. Praise it calmly, "Good hush," then leave the room again. If the pup stays quiet, wait one minute, return, praise and let it out. If it barks, don't let it out until it stops.

When you let your pup out of the crate after this lesson, take it to the potty spot right away and give it a chance to go. If the crate lesson was at all upsetting for the dog, it probably now needs to eliminate.

Repeat the crate-training lesson later that day. Each time, leave your pup closed in the crate a few minutes longer. When it can be quiet in the crate for thirty minutes with you in the house, it's time to leave and go out.

Nighttime Use of Crate

A crate is a cozy private bedroom for your dog. When confined to its crate at night, a dog will be safe and out of trouble. An uncrated dog with the run of the house can wreak havoc while the family sleeps unaware. Potty messes, chewed corners, spilled plants, soiled furniture—imagine all the things your pup could get into in eight unsupervised hours. Confining your pup at night to a clean, comfortable crate will keep it safe and your furnishings intact.

> **MIDNIGHT POTTY**
>
> Get up when your pup wakes you at night and take it to the elimination place. The fewer accidents you let your pup have, day or night, the sooner its housetraining will be complete. Each time the puppy uses its designated elimination area, it mentally links that place with relief and praise. Memories of success accumulate, and when your pup feels the urge to go, it will remember where it went before. Each successful incident helps the pup form the clean habits you want it to have. Final result— clean dog, happy owner.

Before you close your dog in its crate for the night, be sure you take it to eliminate one last time. You may have to wake your puppy to do this, but if you neglect to take the pup to eliminate before you go to bed, you'll have to take it later. Worse yet, the pup may wake and whine and you might sleep right through its pleas. If this occurs, you are sure to awaken to a mess in the morning.

Dogs, being the social creatures they are, like to sleep together in a common area with the rest of the pack. If you put your pup's crate in your bedroom at night, the dog will feel secure and happy to be near you. You are also more likely to hear it if it calls out to you in the middle of the night.

Daytime Use of Crate

When you're home during the day, your pup should spend as much time with you as possible. A good way to keep it from wandering off to soil the carpet is to leash the puppy to your belt. Let it follow you around like a shadow. When you walk, it walks. When you stop, it stops. When you stand at the sink to wash dishes, the pup lies on the floor by your feet. It stays within your reach, so it's impossible for it to do anything wrong without you noticing and correcting it.

When you are unable to supervise for an hour or so, put your pup in its crate to chew on a bone or snooze. Be sure always to give your dog the chance to eliminate before closing it in its crate. When you release it, take it immediately to the elimination area, stand by and praise success.

Alternative Confinement Options

If your pup must be alone all day while everyone is away at work or school, don't leave it in the crate. A safely fenced and sheltered outdoor area can be a good place for your pup when you are away at work. Make certain the fence is secure so your pup won't escape and so other animals can't get in and harm it. It's risky leaving a puppy unattended outdoors, even in a well-fenced yard. Dangers include poisonous plants, insects, snakes, teasing kids and dognappers. Be advised that even if you have a lovely yard for your pup, it may be safer in the house when nobody is home.

If you hope to avoid potty accidents, an unhousetrained puppy must not be allowed free run of the house, even when you are home. If your pup is alone all day, use an exercise pen or puppy corral to confine it instead of a crate. The crate is only big enough to comfortably sleep in. At night that's fine, in fact, that's exactly what you want, but during the daytime a crate should not be used for more that a few hours. There isn't enough space in a crate to give your pup the environment it needs during the day. There is no room to play, and obviously no place to go potty. If you are

> ### WRONGFUL USE OF CRATE
>
> It's unfair to crate a puppy for the night and then lock it up again all day while you go to work. A crate-den is a safe and cozy bed and can be a big help during house-training, but it is not a storage unit or time capsule for your puppy. Owners can unwittingly cause serious behavior and health problems by overusing the crate.
>
> The rule of thumb for daytime crate use is no more than one hour of crate time per day for each month of a pup's age (up to 5 months). No dog of any age should be left in its crate longer than five hours during the day.

When you can't supervise your pup, put it in its crate for a limited time. Be sure to take it out to eliminate before you confine it.

trying to housetrain your pup, it needs an appropriate elimination area in its daytime confinement pen.

SAFETY CHECK FROM PUP'S EYE-VIEW

A puppy playpen or corral must be safety-checked before leaving the pup alone. A bored puppy can be very destructive, so make sure your pup's corral will actually keep it out of trouble. Get down on your hands and knees with your eyes at the same level as your pup's. Now look around, the scenery is different. You are seeing things more from your pup's view. Is there anything you can see that sticks out or hangs down? If so, your pup will want to chew or pull on those items. Find a way to keep temptations to a minimum while your pup is immature. Move precious keepsakes to higher ground or to another room until your pup grows into a dignified adult.

SETTING UP THE PUP'S CORRAL AREA

Put the pup's bed, food, water and toys at one end of the corral area. At the opposite end, spread overlapping newspapers or puddle pads to serve as the potty area. At first, you'll have to cover the whole floor of the corral with papers. As the pup takes itself farther from its bed to eliminate, gradually clear away the papers between the bed and the potty area. Don't be in too much of a hurry about this step, or you'll slow your pup's progress by causing it to make mistakes on the nonpapered floor.

Until your pup is housetrained, it will spend time in its playpen when you are home as well as when you're gone. If its corral is centrally located, the pup will receive the socialization and attention it needs. In the kitchen, your pup will be with the family and will have many more chances to meet guests.

Two-Way

Communication

When discussing the subject of brainpower, some experts point to human communication as proof of our superiority over other animals. We do use more complicated ways to exchange messages than any other species. Human beings have signed, scribed and spoken our thoughts in thousands of different languages  since our journey on this planet began. No other creatures we know of have done this. Yet, in spite of our "superior" language capabilities, we regularly miscommunicate. Dogs rarely do.

Dogs live in packs, family groupings that nurture and protect one another. Adult dogs teach the puppies the pack rules. They learn who to play with, how to find food, when to be quiet and where to eliminate. Dogs are social creatures and communicate clearly with their own kind through body postures and vocal tones. Tones are very important—no one would mistake a whimper for a growl, but the canine stance and facial expression speaks volumes.

Body Language

For good communication with your dog, it is important that you understand what it's saying when it "speaks" with its body. When you understand dog language, you'll have better success with your dog's training. Communication is a two-way exchange. Understanding dog language is as important for the owner as learning human language is for the dog.

Our dogs' natural understanding of body signals can help us train them or can set us back, depending on how clearly we can body-speak. Our dogs read leadership in our posture when we stand tall with head held high. When we stoop or slouch, our posture conveys submission. A dog will not obey one who is submissive to it.

This dog's posture—head held high and tail awag—conveys its good feeling about itself.

Altitude Equals Attitude

When two dogs communicate, their postures convey important information. Battles can be fought or truces granted solely on the basis of postural signals. The height at which a dog holds its head and tail immediately communicate its attitude. High carriage signals confidence, dominance and leadership. Head up, ears up, fur up, tail up—that's the posture of the dog who would be king. Low carriage indicates insecurity, submission and noncombativeness. Head down, ears down, eyes down, belly and tail low—that's the underdog look. A dog may mix these postural signals when at play, but will not do so in nonplay situations.

Postural Clues

Understanding the meanings of your dog's postures can also help you win the battle of the puddle. When your dog is getting ready to eliminate, it will display a specific set of postures. The sooner you can learn to read these signals, the cleaner your floor will stay.

A young puppy feels the urge to eliminate and may start to sniff the ground and walk in a circle. If the pup is very young, it may simply squat and go. You must be vigilant to notice postural signs. A young puppy won't have much time between feeling the urge and actually eliminating, so you'll have to be quick to note its postural clues and intercept your pup in time.

DEFECATION POSTURE

When a puppy is getting ready to defecate, it may run urgently back and forth, or turn in a circle while sniffing or starting to squat. If defecation is imminent, the pup's anus may protrude or open slightly. When it starts to go, the pup will squat and hunch its back, its tail sticking straight out behind. There is no mistaking this posture; nothing else looks like this. If your pup takes this position, take it to the potty area. Hurry! You may have to carry it to get there in time.

URINATION POSTURES

All young puppies, male or female, squat to piddle. If you are housetraining a pup under 4 months of age, regardless of its sex, watch for the beginnings of a squat as the signal to rush the pup to the potty area. Pups from 3 to 6 months have a few seconds more between the urge and the act than younger ones do. The older your pup, the more time you'll have to get it to the potty place after it begins the body signals that alert you to its need.

LEG LIFTING

Most adult females will squat to urinate, although a few with dominant attitudes manage to lift a hind leg while squatting. Adult males usually lift a rear leg when urinating, which allows them to mark territory more efficiently by aiming the stream against an upright object. Some will mark an object then turn around, hike the other leg and mark again.

Male pups may not cock a leg to pee until they reach adolescence. An occasional precocious male might start lifting its leg at 2 or 3 months of age. Male puppies usually begin urinating with the leg raised after watching a grown-up doggie friend pee that way, then copy its style. Once the leg lifting habit is in place, male dogs very seldom revert to squatting for urination.

A male dog will start lifting a leg to urinate around the time that it reaches adolescence.

Previously Kenneled Dogs

Some adolescent or adult dogs that have been kenneled all their lives and have never been in a house may eliminate without a qualm anywhere they happen to be. You will have to watch this dog very closely. It has no idea that potty on the floor is wrong. Treat this dog as you would a small pup, giving ample opportunity to eliminate in the correct area and praising the dog's success.

Some mature kennel dogs no longer care if the den smells of waste; these dogs are difficult to housetrain because their earlier habits are so strong. Watch the dog's body signals carefully, leash it to your belt rather than letting it wander the house and crate it at night. If you can prevent it from engaging in its old potty habits for about three months, it will probably become trained to be clean in the house. If you don't work hard at this, though, the dog may soil your house repeatedly.

Other ex-kennel dogs have, for some reason, strong inhibitions against eliminating indoors. Maybe they are just sick and tired of living in their own stench and welcome the opportunity to live in a clean home. These former kennel dogs may become very anxious when they're indoors and feel the need to eliminate. They may whine, pace, bark or go to the door. If you notice any of these behaviors, immediately take the dog to the designated area for potty.

Wandering Off to Eliminate

An adolescent or adult that isn't housetrained might, instead of going to the door that leads out, head for a remote room of the house. It is looking for a way to get farther from its den area to eliminate, but it will end up displeasing you by using the parlor or guest bedroom as its potty area. This is an honest mistake. Many houses are large enough that a dog might think an unused room is the equivalent of an indoor backyard.

If you see your dog starting to wander off down the hall, do not assume it's looking for a secluded place to rest. It's more likely looking for a secluded place to eliminate. Don't fall for this trick; wake up and read the dog's body language.

Why Accidents Happen

Many a potty accident has happened because the dog was unable to communicate its need. When feeling the need to eliminate, a pup might rush to the door that leads to the potty area. If that door is closed, the way to success, relief and praise is blocked. The pup may stand by the door, staring hopefully at the doorknob, wishing the door would open. If someone let it outside at this point, the pup would be happy to eliminate in its designated area. But alas, no one appears and the door stays shut. Finally, unable to hold it any longer, the pup puddles by the door.

The puppy went to the door intending to go to its potty spot, but the door wouldn't open. If only the pup had known how to let someone know of its plight.

Teaching Your Dog to Ask to Go Out

There is an easy way to teach a dog to ask to go potty. Your pup can learn to ring a bell with its paw or nose when it wants out.

THE POTTY BELL

The potty bell should be loud enough that you can hear it from the next room, yet small enough that a pup can easily ring it. A small brass bell or string of sleigh bells would work nicely. Hang the bell from the doorknob of the door to the potty area. The bell should hang at about the height of the pup's nose.

Each time you take your dog to its outdoor elimination area, ring the bell. While you're on your way to the door with your dog say, "Let's go out, go potty." Just before you open the door, ring the bell. You don't have to try to make the dog ring it, just ring it yourself and open the door. The pup will learn to ring the bell itself by imitating you.

Dogs think in a linear way: Whatever happens just before an event, causes the event. If the bell rings and then the door opens, the bell must have caused the door to open. After a few dozen times of hearing the potty bell and then having you open the door, the pup will decide to give it a try.

The puppy will experimentally tap the bell with its nose or paw. Upon hearing this sweetest of music, you should rush to open the door for your wonderful puppy. The dog notes that the experiment worked and will probably try it again the next time. In any-where from four days to two weeks, your dog will make that connection between the bell and the door opening, and, from then on, it can ask to go out when it needs to.

FALSE ALARMS

Once it figures out how to call you to open the door for it, the pup might try using the potty bell when it wants out for play. Discourage this. Escort your dog out to the potty area when it rings the bell. Don't allow it to play or to wander off. Wait with the pup for a reasonable time and, if it doesn't go, take it back inside. The potty bell is such a valuable communication signal; it must not be used for false alarms.

Teaching Your Dog to "Go" on Command

Many dog owners are happy enough if their dogs just make it out the door before eliminating. That's fine for some, but why not hold higher standards? Teach your dog to eliminate when and where you command. At home, an elimination command can speed up trips to the potty spot. Away from home, the command can in-form your dog where the designated area is. Teaching an elimination command is so easy and useful that it's surprising more owners don't do so.

There is no "official" command for elimination, so simply choose one you feel comfortable with. "Go potty" and "Get busy" are popular; many guide dogs are trained to "Park," and more than one bright little pup has learned to obey the scientific-sounding "Urinate." Some people use the same word for the pup's elimination as they would for their children. Select a word you don't mind saying in public, because sometimes you'll have to.

When you take your dog to eliminate, say the command word. When the dog produces, praise it softly using the command word in a praise phrase (i.e., "Good do business"). Soon it will go whenever and wherever you command.

Increased Maturity

After 3 months of age, most pups get sufficient warning when it's time to eliminate that they can walk away from bed and bowl before they go potty. A pup that age may grasp the idea that there's a special place it's supposed to eliminate. When the pup feels nature's call, it may look around urgently, trying to remember how to get to the potty area. The easier you make it, the quicker housetraining will proceed.

By 3 months of age, some pups already go to the door to be let out. You will still need to coax, remind and facilitate, especially when your puppy first wakes up, when it's very excited or when it pauses in play.

Even if your pup doesn't quite make it to the area before letting go, don't scold. Instead, praise its honorable intentions. Good housetraining isn't about punishing a dog when it fails; it's about encouraging it to succeed.

Preventing Accidents

If you see your pup about to potty somewhere other than the designated area, interrupt it immediately. Say "Wait, wait, wait!" or "No, no, no!" to startle it into stopping. Carry the pup, if it's still small enough, or take its collar and lead it to the correct area. Once your dog is in the potty area, give the command to eliminate. Use a friendly voice for the command, then wait patiently for it to produce. The pup may be tense because you've just startled it and may have to relax a bit before it's able to eliminate. When it does its job, include the command word in the praise you give (i.e., "Good potty").

Finding an Accident After the Fact

Some trainers say a dog can't remember having eliminated, even a few moments after it has done so. This is not true. The fact is that urine and feces carry a dog's unique scent, which it (and every other dog) can instantly recognize. Dogs use urine and feces to mark their territory, which would be useless if their individual scent was not contained therein. When they smell their own urine or feces, dogs can and do remember it's theirs. So, if you happen upon a potty mistake after the fact, you can still use it to teach your dog.

USING EVIDENCE TO TEACH

When you find evidence of a potty mistake, take a paper towel and your dog to the scene of the crime.

Never push the dog's nose into the mess as trainers did many years ago. That's confusing to the dog if you're trying to teach it to be clean. Moreover, it's disgusting and you'll have a stinky dog to clean up as well as the mess on your floor. Just hold the dog near the accident, point to the evidence and say "No potty here!" Then, using the paper towel, pick up the pile or sop up some of the puddle and take the dog and evidence to the proper elimination spot. Drop the poop or smear the pee on the ground (hide the paper towel or it will distract the pup) and command your dog to eliminate.

By circling and sniffing, the pup is indicating that it wants to get outside.

If your pup sniffs at the evidence, praise it calmly. If the accident happened very recently, your dog may not have to go yet, but wait with it a few minutes anyway. If it goes potty, praise it. Afterwards, go finish cleaning up the mess.

Unable to get its owner's attention, the pup urinates on the floor.

SHOULD YOUR PUP SEE YOU CLEAN UP?

Some trainers say never to let a pup see you clean up its messes. Others say you should make it watch. So what should you do? Actually, it doesn't seem to make much difference with most pups. Just do what's convenient. If the pup does watch, though, and comes over to sniff and see what you're doing, take that opportunity to tell it again that this was a "bad potty." Don't go overboard with this, just make the statement in a mildly disgusted voice.

On discovering the accident, the owner takes the puppy to the scene, tells it, "No potty here," and wipes some urine up with a paper towel.

Accidents and Punishments

The old-fashioned way of housetraining involved punishing a dog's mistakes, even

The owner takes the pup and towel outside to reinforce good habits.

The owner then smears some urine on the ground. She praises the pup as it sniffs.

before it knew what it was supposed to do. Puppies were punished for breaking rules they didn't understand about functions they couldn't control. This was not fair.

While your dog is new to housetraining, there is no need or excuse for punishing its mistakes. The owner's job is to take the dog to the potty area just before it needs to go, especially with pups under 3 months. If you aren't watching your pup closely enough, and it has an accident, don't punish the puppy for your failure to anticipate its needs.

Over the years, people have devised all sorts of punishment techniques to use on their dogs. Most involve hitting the dog in one way or another. Some trainers advise spanking with a newspaper so the dog won't fear your hand. Some advise a hard slap under the dog's chin so it won't see the blow coming. Others recommend shaking the dog, throwing it on the ground, tossing a can of pennies at it or squirting it with water.

None of these punishments are good or necessary for housetraining. A pup is unlikely to make any connection between these punishments and having relieved itself earlier. If the owner had been paying better attention, the pup might have successfully made it to the potty spot. A dog will learn faster when you help it than when you hurt or frighten it.

Spanking, hitting, shaking or scaring a puppy for having a housetraining accident is confusing and counterproductive. Spend your energy instead on positive forms of teaching.

DO NOT PUNISH ERRORS

Help your puppy get to the potty place on time. Praise its success when it produces. Do not punish elimination errors. It doesn't do any good to punish a pup for a behavior it isn't yet able to control. As your dog matures and gains control of body functions, it will take itself to the potty place when it needs to go. Until then, take the time to teach your pup where you want it to eliminate.

chapter 9

A Schedule
May Help

"What goes up must come down" is the well-known saying about gravity. Elimination, which is just as sure a force, has its own pithy proverb, "What goes in must come out." While that is an oversimplified description of digestion and elimination, it is, nonetheless, accurate. What is eaten, and when it is digested, controls the timing of your pup's elimination. Allow your pup free access to water all day. It must drink frequently to  stay healthy. Water intake should not be limited, except at night. Regulating a dog's access to food, however, is safe and will help your pup's elimination times be more predictable.

The clear relationship between your puppy's intake and output is good news for anyone in the housetraining stages of dog ownership. Controlling when, what and how much your pup eats will make predicting its elimination needs easy. As we know, house-training a pup under 12 weeks of age is largely a matter of getting the pup to the right spot at the right time. Even with older pups and adult dogs, knowing in advance when that "right time" will occur can save numerous cleanups and fruitless trips to the potty area. A feeding and exercise schedule can help your pup learn to be clean. Schedules can also prevent or change some difficult and resistant housetraining problems.

Scheduling Basics

The timing of feeding, sleep, play and potty will differ depending on the age of your pup or dog. Young puppy bodies require more frequent filling and emptying than older pups and adults. Sometimes it might seem that young pups eat, drink and potty so often that there's little time left for play or sleep.

> ### PUP WAKES UP
>
> Puppies tend to be early risers, and when your pup awakens at the crack of dawn you'll have to get up and take it to its elimination area. Patience and understanding are critical—when your dog is an adult, it is as likely to want to sleep in as you are.

Your normal rising and bedtimes may be different than those specified in the following schedule. You may adapt the schedules to fit your own hours by simply adjusting the listed rising time. The intervals between meals and potty times are more important here than what hour your day happens to begin.

EARLY TO RISE

With a new puppy in the home, don't be surprised if your rising time is suddenly a little earlier than you've been accustomed to. Puppies have earned a reputation as very early risers. When your pup wakes you at the crack of dawn, you will have to get up and take it to its elimination spot. Be patient. When your dog is an adult, it may enjoy sleeping in as much as you do.

It's fine to adjust rising times when using these schedules, but you should not adjust the intervals between feedings and potty outings unless your pup's behavior justifies a change. Your puppy can only meet your expectations in housetraining if you help it learn the rules.

The schedules for puppies are devised under the assumption that someone will be home most of the time with the pup. That would be the best scenario, of course, but is not always possible. If you must leave your pup alone during its early housetraining period, be sure to cover the entire floor of its playpen with thick layers of overlapping newspaper. If you come home to messes in the crate or puppy corral, just clean them up. If you were able to be home, your pup would have someone to remind it where to go potty. Be patient—it's still a baby.

CRATE ABUSE

Do not use your pup's sleeping crate to store it while you go off to work your 8-hour shift. A puppy needs to move around and exercise. It needs to play, eat and drink water. And it will need to eliminate. It cannot possibly do all that in a crate. A pup needs a playpen or corral. If you must leave it alone for the day, a crate is too small. Crating a pup for the whole day is abusive. Don't do it.

If you must leave a young pup alone during the day, be sure to cover its entire playpen with newspapers.

A PET SITTER

Owners can sometimes ease the problems of a latchkey pup by having a neighbor or friend look in on the pup at noon and take it to eliminate. A better solution might be hiring a pet sitter to drop by midday. A professional pet sitter will be knowledgeable about companion animals and able to give your pup high-quality care and socialization. Some can even help train your pup in both potty manners and basic obedience. Unlike a neighbor or friend, a professional pet sitter will not become bored taking daily care of your pup. Ask your veterinarian and your dog-owning friends to recommend a good pet sitter.

Schedule for Pup Under 10 Weeks

11 p.m. (Night before)   Lay out easy-on clothes and shoes before going to bed. There will be no time to choose your wardrobe in the morning when you jump out of bed to take your pup to its potty place. And don't forget your house keys!

7:00 a.m.   Get up, take puppy from sleeping crate directly to potty spot. Carry if necessary.

7:15   Clean up night's messes if any.

7:30   Feed and water pup.

7:45   Pick up food bowl. Take pup to potty spot; wait and praise.

8:00   Pup plays around your feet while you drink coffee and prepare breakfast. You'll notice that it has now been one hour since you got up. Finally you have this short moment to take care of yourself and, maybe, the rest of the family. Console yourself that, if you've been following this schedule so far, you shouldn't have had any new messes to clean up for the past hour.

8:15   Potty time again.

8:30   Put pup in crate for nap.

10:00   Pup wakes, out to potty.

10:15   Puppy in corral with safe toys to chew and play with.

As you watch your pup at play, observe its behavior. Learn to recognize what it does immediately before eliminating. Any sudden searching, sniffing or circling behavior is a likely sign it has to go. As soon as you see that, carry or lead the pup to its potty spot and calmly tell it to eliminate. Praise its success.

If you miss the moment and arrive some time after the flood, do not scold or punish. It's not the pup's fault you were late.

10:45   Potty.

11:00   Playtime. Throw or roll a ball and encourage your pup to chase after it and bring it back to you. Play gentle games and teach your pup to play without biting hands and clothes. Interactive play with people is important for growing pups. Sufficient exercise is important, too, promoting a strong body, healthy appetite and, yes, regular elimination.

11:30   Potty time again.

11:45   Food and fresh water.

12:00 p.m.   Pick up food bowl. Take pup to potty spot.

12:15   Crate pup for nap with a safe chew toy.

2:00   Potty.

2:15   Snack and beginner obedience training practice.

Some pups like their kibbled dry dog food so well that you can use it as treat lures and rewards for training. This is better, nutritionally speaking, than rich or salty treats. The customary food will not upset a pup's digestive system, as certain treat foods may. Some doggie snack foods can cause excessive thirst and loose stools. These are conditions that you will want to avoid while your pup is in housetraining. If your pup has an adverse reaction to treat foods, stick with its regular dog food kibble for rewards.

A puppy will need to eliminate frequently, and you will want to give it many opportunities to do so.

2:45   Potty.

3:00   Pup in corral with safe toys and chews for solitary play and/or nap.

4:15   Potty.

4:30   Make pup a part of household activities by making it your shadow.

Loop a 6-foot leash through your belt and attach the other end to your pup's collar or harness. Watch and guide your pup's behavior. When it needs to eliminate, you'll be right there to notice, take it to the right spot in time and praise its good job.

5:00   Feed and freshen water.

5:15 Potty.

5:30 Pup may play nearby (either leashed or corralled) while you prepare your evening meal.

6:00 Potty, then crate while you eat and clean up after dinner.

7:00 Potty.

7:15 Leashed or closely watched, this is a good time for the pup to play and socialize with family and visitors for a few hours.

Offer the pup water occasionally throughout the evening. A dog needs water to digest its food.

Take the pup to potty spot whenever it acts like it needs to go.

9:00 Last water of the evening.

9:15 Potty. Crate pup or keep it as close as a shadow. Do not let it wander off unescorted. You've done so well so far today, don't give the pup an opportunity to make a mess for you to clean up now, at this hour!

10:45 Last chance to potty.

11:00 Put pup to bed in crate for the night. Go to bed yourself and get some rest. You've earned it!

3:00 or 4:00 a.m. Your pup awakes and has to eliminate. Take it to the potty spot and make sure it does everything it has to do. Then re-crate the pup with a safe, quiet chew toy (preferably the type with an internal hollow for food that will hold the pup's interest for awhile). Go back to sleep until your alarm goes off.

You'll notice that this schedule calls for you to take your pup to the potty area about fifteen times a day. That may actually be more than your pup really needs to go, but you should take it that often at first. After keeping track for a few days, you'll start to notice your pup's own digestive/eliminative body rhythms. Some pups eliminate more often than others. As you learn your pup's needs, you can adjust the schedule to meet them.

Schedule for Pups 10 Weeks to 6 Months

As pups mature, they eat and eliminate less often than when they were small. As your pup's exterior expands, its insides grow larger as well. Stomach, bladder and intestines increase in capacity. The 5-month-old pup eats bigger meals and can hold its urine and feces longer than it could at 3 months. That means less frequent, but larger, puddles and poops as the dog grows.

The schedule for a pup from 10 weeks to 6 months requires less frequent feeding and potty visits, but more play and socializing time. During this period, you should keep your puppy with you as much as possible. It needs to learn about all the amazing things in its world. The pup will learn to follow and respect you as its leader during this period. Give it good opportunities to do so by daily shadow-leashing the fast-growing pup to your belt. Not only will you be right there to prevent potty accidents, you'll also be available to guide the pup's behavior around people, pets and property.

> ### BE PATIENT WITH YOUR PUP
>
> If it's impossible to be with your puppy during the day, realize that its housetraining will progress more slowly than if you were there to coach. Punishing your pup for soiling its playpen area while you were away is completely inappropriate. It's not your puppy's fault if it soils its area, then tracks through it and makes a stinky mess. It's only a baby. What could anyone realistically expect of a baby left at home without supervision?

7:00 a.m.   Get up, take puppy from sleeping crate to potty spot.

7:15   Clean up night's messes if any.

7:30   Feed and water pup.

7:45   Pick up food bowl. Take pup to potty spot; wait and praise.

8:00   Pup plays around your feet while you eat breakfast.

9:00   Potty.

9:15   Play and obedience practice.

10:00   Potty.

10:15 Puppy in corral with safe toys for solitary play and/or nap.

11:30 Potty.

11:45 Food and fresh water.

12:00 p.m. Pick up food bowl. Take pup to potty spot.

12:15 Pup in corral.

1:00 Potty.

1:15 Let pup shadow you, leashed to your belt.

3:30 Potty.

3:45 Pup in corral with safe toys for solitary play and/or nap.

4:45 Potty.

Let your adult dog out of its crate and take it to its elimination spot first thing in the morning.

5:00 Feed and freshen water.

5:15 Potty.

5:30 Pup may play either leashed or corralled while you prepare and eat your evening meal.

7:00 Potty.

7:15 Leashed or closely watched, pup plays and socializes with family.

9:15 Potty.

10:45 Last chance to potty.

11:00 Crate pup for the night.

Schedule for Adolescent and Adult Dogs

An older pup or adult dog that is not yet housetrained must be watched and regulated as closely as a young pup. It may not have to eliminate as often as a baby pup, but if an adolescent or adult dog knows no manners, it may potty wherever it happens to be when the urge strikes. As you learn your dog's habits and rhythms, it will be fairly easy to anticipate its needs.

7:00 a.m. Get up, take dog from crate to potty spot.

7:30   Feed and water.

7:45   Pick up food bowl. Take dog to potty spot.

8:00   Allow dog to play or lounge in room with you. Provide chew toys. Leash to belt if it tries to wander away.

10:00   Potty.

10:15   Play and obedience practice, then leash to belt.

11:45   Potty.

12:00 p.m.   Feed and freshen water.

12:15   Pick up food bowl. Take dog to potty spot.

12:45   Solitary play in corral or outdoor fenced yard.

2:45   Potty.

3:00   Let dog shadow you, leashed to your belt.

5:00   Feed and freshen water.

5:15   Pick up bowl and take dog to potty area.

5:30   Leash dog to belt while you prepare and eat your meal.

7:15   Potty.

7:30   Closely watched, dog plays off leash and socializes with family.

9:30   Potty.

10:45   Last chance to potty.

11:00   Crate for the night.

> ### MEALS VERSUS SELF-FEEDING
>
> Although many owners allow their adolescent and adult dogs to free feed, this is not appropriate if you're trying to housetrain. Regular meals mean regular elimination for dogs of any age. Some adult dogs do quite well on one daily meal but most professionals recommend feeding twice a day.

Your dog's body rhythms may require changes in the schedule that you devise. Don't let a rigid schedule get in the way of your dog's housetraining success.

Use these schedules as a basic plan or template to help prevent potty accidents. Meanwhile, use your own powers of observation to discover how best to modify the basic schedule to fit your dog's own unique needs. Each dog is an individual and will have its own body rhythms.

Special
Housetraining

part three

Problems

chapter 10

Recurring

Elimination

Problems

Some elimination problems can occur repeatedly, despite attempts to convince a dog of the error of its ways. Instead of giving in to frustration and anger with your dog, try to decipher the causes of recurring elimination problems. Persistent potty mistakes often stem from ages-old instinctive canine behavior.

Marking

Our dogs' wild ancestors never needed brass nameplates or numbers to mark their home addresses. Instead, they mark their property with urine. The instinct to mark territory this way has been passed down to our domestic dogs. When a dog wants to mark its trail or property, it urinates, leaving its own distinctive scent. This lets any animal that follows know that the path has been traveled or the territory claimed.

A dog with the run of the house while you're away can get pretty comfortable lounging on your bed or in your favorite chair. To let other animals know those comfy spots are already claimed, the dog may pee on a corner or two. It isn't necessarily "jumping" your claim, and it may not mind a bit sharing those comfy spots with you when you're home. It's just that you're not around much and someone has to keep the wolves away. Right? So the dog marks. You come home and wash it off. It marks again. You wash it off again. You feel like you are at war with your dog, but all it's doing is renewing the scent mark to protect the territory from outsiders.

This handy marking system worked well for wild wolves, but it creates a problem with domestic dogs. Owners become frustrated and angry with dogs that urine-mark. This perfectly natural canine behavior can be very messy and destructive for the owner. Marking must be controlled if the dog and its human family are to live together without major conflicts.

MANAGING MARKING

A dog that marks must be given plenty of outdoor exercise, preferably on leash, so the owner can direct the dog to mark appropriate objects, like rocks and trees. That will help it by giving it an outlet for marking behavior of which the owner approves. The dog must also be prevented from marking inappropriately, as when in the house.

Dogs that mark when left alone cannot be allowed the run of the house. They need closer confinement. A crate is suitable if the dog doesn't have to be in it for more than five hours, and not every day. For longer confinement, a crate is not humane. To stay healthy a dog

> ### CURES FOR BOREDOM-RELATED ELIMINATION
>
> Ask a friend or hire a professional pet sitter to walk your dog once or twice a day. Your dog will get needed exercise, have opportunities to eliminate in approved places and will be less bored than just waiting at home for you. Bored dogs have nothing better to do than chew, bark, mark and mess while you're gone. Less time spent alone can have a very positive effect on a dog's behavior and attitude.
>
> Find interesting activities to share with your dog when you are home. Watching TV reruns together is not enough. Find something more active to do with your dog. Go for walks in new places, play games, teach tricks—exercise your dog's mind and its muscles. Improving your dog/owner interaction is one of the best ways to decrease behavior problems of all types.

needs to be able to move around, drink and eliminate. It can't do that while crated, so it will need a pen or fenced yard.

Marking is natural for dogs, but it becomes a real problem when it occurs in the home.

In an ideal world, we would each have a lovely fenced yard for our dogs to enjoy while we're away. Not everyone does, of course, so other options must be explored. An exercise pen indoors would work well for a small dog, but may be too cramped for a larger one. Remember that your dog may urine-mark while it's in its

indoor pen and may thereby pee on your floor or furniture. Take the dog's marking problem into account as you set up its confinement area. You may have to use tarps or plastic to keep the dog from wetting things next to the ex-pen.

Some dogs that mark do so more when they're bored and underexercised. Check into having a friend or a professional pet sitter come walk your dog once or twice a day. That way, your dog will get exercise, have opportunities to urinate in approved places and be much less bored. This may help a great deal.

Spite?

Dogs are not generally a spiteful lot, so when owners name that as the motive in unacceptable elimination, they are usually mistaken.

Dogs may express dominance and property ownership by marking with urine or feces. This behavior could easily be interpreted as spiteful by an owner at war with his or her dog's instincts.

What is often viewed as spite urination usually occurs while the owner is away and the dog is loose in the house alone. In a typical scenario, the dog is housetrained and has the run of the home. The owner returns from work one day to find dog urine or feces in inappropriate places. The owner scolds the dog and thoroughly cleans the soiled spots. But then the same thing happens the next day and again a few days later. Spite? There are more likely causes that should be explored.

Health Problem

One cause of urination on the master's bed may be that the dog has a bladder infection. A dog with this condition finds urination very painful and tries to hold back as long as possible. Finally, it cannot help but urinate, so the dog seeks a place of comfort in its misery. It may go into the master's bedroom, hoping the deity-person's special bed will protect it from pain as it urinates.

A dog that would do this usually is one with a strong, positive attachment to the owner. Hopefully, the owner will realize that the dog is seeking comfort in its pain rather than being spiteful. The poor dog needs medical attention, not punishment.

Dominance Problem

Dominance is a natural canine trait that is occasionally expressed through marking behavior. The typical case is an adult dog, usually (but not always) a male, that marks with urine or feces while the owner is away. This is natural behavior, though detestable, and has little to do with spite.

A dog's urine and feces carry its unique scent, and when deposited on an object or territory, marks that property as the dog's own. A dominant dog is a social and economic climber that will normally claim as much real estate as it can. Dogs "own" property by either burying it where nobody else will find it or by marking it with urine or feces.

Problems occur when a dominant dog starts claiming the owner's belongings as its own. This is most common in latchkey dogs that are home alone all day while their owner works. Try to imagine this situation from the dog's point of view. You're not home as much as the dog is, so it's really the dog's turf, not yours. You just sleep there at night and maybe hang around on weekends. If the latchkey dog marks property while you're gone, it may actually believe it's marking its own territory, not yours.

MANAGING DOMINANCE MARKING

If a dog eliminates because it is ill, of course the solution is to have the veterinarian treat it. It is not always easy to tell when a dog is unwell, so if your housetrained adult starts urinating in the house, have the veterinarian check for health problems before you assume that the behavior is emotionally based.

Some adult dogs in a poor relationship with their owners do mark to dominate them. In these cases, there are usually other clues besides wrongful elimination that the dog is attempting to dominate the owner. Often, these dogs will ignore commands, push past the owner in a doorway, pull hard on leash when walked and may play roughly enough to hurt. Dogs like this also may growl at their owners and use intimidation to get their own way. This can become dangerous. Owners of dogs that are trying to dominate people should seek help from a professional trainer with experience handling dominance problems.

Dogs that are home alone all day may perceive the property as their own (rather than yours). This can lead to dominance marking.

Submissive Urination

Submissive urination can be viewed as the "opposite" of marking. The dog pees, not because it's dominant, but because it is submissive. This behavior is seen in male pups but is more common in immature females. Some dogs keep the piddling habit into adulthood, but it usually is not as extreme as in puppyhood.

In some young pups, the urethral valves are not sufficiently developed to hold back urine during times of excitement. Maturity will alleviate the problem. True submissive urination is an expression of respect, not a problem with underdeveloped valves.

If a pup piddles at your feet when it says hello, when you scold it or if you bend or reach over it, that pup is urinating submissively. It does this to let you know you are its hero. Try to feel flattered. The pup doesn't intend to irritate you with its display, but rather make peace with you. It is trying to show you that it's just a wet-bottomed pup with no desire to be your rival.

MANAGING SUBMISSIVE URINATION

You cannot discourage submissive urination by punishing or scolding. By responding angrily, the dog will simply try harder to convince you of its submission. It can only do that by peeing more. You could drown before you'd stop a submissive piddler by punishing it.

By urinating in response to your arrival or attention, a pup is showing its respect for you.

The best technique in managing a submissive piddler is to keep everything low-key. Don't greet the pup or even acknowledge it until you've been home for ten minutes. Don't look at, talk to or bend to pet your pup until it's less excited.

Greet the pup outdoors, if possible. Then if it wets, it's not a problem. Walk around as you greet it rather than stopping to pet the dog. Speak quietly and avoid high-pitched baby talk. The more mellow the greeting, the less likely your pup is to pee when it sees you.

Hiding Elimination

Some owners punish harshly for potty accidents, and this is a mistake. Punishment can scare the pup and cause it to fear the owner's anger, while not understanding exactly what the anger is about. If the dog figures out that your wrath had something to do with potty, it may do its best to never let you see it eliminate.

This can create several problems. Not realizing there is a "right" place to eliminate, the dog may think the owner wants it never to potty at all. A dog with that idea will refuse to eliminate in front of its owner, so escorted trips to the elimination area will bear no fruit. Because this dog cannot eliminate while the owner is present, it must wait until it can be alone. This dog may sneak off to leave messes behind furniture or in little-used rooms of the house.

At first, the owner may not realize that this sneaking behavior is happening. The odor may be noticeable, but no evidence will be in view. Only when a guest arrives to use the extra bedroom or when the furniture is rearranged will the hidden deeds be discovered. The rug in the spare room or behind the sofa will be spotted like an appaloosa, and there may be weeks' worth of petrified poops. Upon discovering the crime scene, some owners fly into a rage and severely punish the pup. Others simply sigh, clean up the mess and hope for better behavior in the future. Neither of these owner behaviors will help change the dog's habit.

To correct hiding, stay with your dog in its elimination area after it uses the right spot. Praise calmly, letting your dog know that what it has done is just swell.

TO CORRECT HIDING

If your dog has been hiding its elimination from you, there is a reason for that. Your dog is trying its best not to give you any reason to be angry about its elimination. If it knew a way to please you with potty behavior, the dog would have no reason to hide its pees and poops.

To cure potty hiding behavior, you'll have to convince your dog that there is a praiseworthy place to eliminate. The best way to do this is start over again with housetraining, as if you had just brought the pup home.

First and foremost, if you have been punishing your dog for elimination mistakes, quit that immediately. The dog probably doesn't understand the rules you're trying to enforce, so you'll only confuse and frighten it with punishment. This will delay learning and be frustrating for both you and your pup.

When you are home and can watch your pup closely, it can be free in whatever room you're in. If you are too involved to watch the pup every second, leash it to your belt and let it follow you like a shadow. If it tries to sneak off, the leash will prevent it, but you'll get the clue that the pup has to potty.

Tell the pup in a friendly voice that it's time to go to its elimination place, then take it there and wait for it to go. When it does, praise the pup calmly and admire its puddle or pile. Stay in the potty area for about five minutes after the pup is finished, occasionally giving more calm praise. This will let it know you are not upset by it eliminating there.

Don't clean up the urine or feces right away or the dog may think you didn't approve after all. Let the poop or pee remain until after the pup has been put to bed that night. Then clean up all but a tiny bit of the elimination. Leave only enough to scent the spot for the next day.

A Potty Pen for a Modest Dog

The dog that hides its elimination is usually a sensitive soul. It hides because it fears displeasing you. The dog may be worried that if you see it eliminate, you'll punish it. When you take it to the potty area, this dog may be unable to produce with you standing nearby. If that happens, use an ex-pen indoors for a potty area or a fenced area outdoors where you'll be able to see the pup without looming over it.

When it's time for the puppy to eliminate, put it in the potty pen and then stand sufficiently far away that it's not bothered by your presence. Watch for the pup to eliminate. After you see it go potty, wait a minute or so before returning to praise and admire its job.

Leave the elimination right where it is; don't clean up until your pup has had several successes. Cover each poop or puddle with more sheets of newspaper after you've praised the pup, but wait until it's in bed for the night before removing the mess from its potty area. Clean the area, but leave a scent reminder for the dog's first trip to its potty pen in the morning.

Mounting

Mounting is a male sexual posture and it is also a normal, but impolite, gesture of dominance. A dog may mount objects like pillows or stuffed toys, or it may mount other dogs, or even human members of its social circle. Both males and females mount as a sign of dominance, even those that have been neutered.

Sometimes a urethral infection or other irritation of the urinary tract can cause mounting behavior. A dog with a urinary health problem may feel pain or itching that is temporarily relieved when it mounts and rubs itself.

Managing Mounting

When mounting is caused by a dominant nature, the cure is behavioral intervention. When it's caused by an infection or irritation, the cure is medical intervention. If your dog mounts often, take it to the veterinary clinic to be checked for urinary tract problems. You will not be able to stop this behavior simply through training if it is caused by a health problem.

Urinary tract infections and irritations can be cured with swift and proper treatment. Once firmly entrenched, however, infections can be difficult to eradicate and may cause permanent kidney damage. If your dog is mounting and rubbing, get its health checked right away.

Breed-Related Problems

Some elimination problems are caused by hereditary factors. These may be structural or chemical abnormalities that cause lack of control. The chapter on health-related problems goes into greater detail, but listed here are some common conditions and the breeds at genetic risk.

Urolithiasis   Cocker Spaniel, Dachshund, Dalmatian, Miniature Poodle, Shih Tzu, Yorkshire Terrier.

Cushing's Disease (hyperadrenocorticism)   Boston Terrier, Boxer, Dachshund, Poodle.

Diabetes Mellitus   Cavalier King Charles Spaniel, Cocker Spaniel, Dachshund, Doberman Pinscher, German Shepherd Dog, Golden Retriever, Labrador Retriever, Pomeranian, Rottweiler, Samoyed.

Managing Breed-Related Problems

The best thing to do about hereditary problems is avoid them by buying dogs only from responsible and knowledgeable breeders. A reputable breeder checks all breeding stock for testable genetic conditions before mating them.

If you already have a dog that has elimination problems stemming from genetic causes, follow your veterinarian's advice. Good medical treatment and home care can lessen the severity of many inherited problems and allow a dog to live a comfortable and happy life.

Toy Breeds

Many toy breed dogs have persistent troubles with housetraining. Each time a dog eliminates in an approved area, the good habit of doing so is fortified. Each time a dog potties in the wrong place, a bad habit is strengthened instead. Toy dogs are certainly not any dirtier or more stubborn than their larger cousins, but, because of their tiny size, it's easier for elimination mistakes to go undiscovered and uncorrected.

Owners must be watchful to catch a pup and take it to its elimination area before it has potty accidents. When the scent of a pup's urine and feces is detectable only in its designated potty place, it will get the idea that that's the place to go. However, if the smell is scattered around in other areas, the pup will not remember which spot is the right one.

With a larger pup or dog, there is no mistaking when there's been a potty accident. The puddle or poop is plenty big to notice. The owner can use that evidence to train, by showing the dog its mistake, scolding mildly, then taking both dog and mess to the correct area to complete the lesson and praise. With toy breed pups, however, the accidental puddle may consist of only about a tablespoon of urine. This tiny amount may disappear into the carpet and remain undiscovered. Owners may have no idea their dog has been peeing all over the place until the house begins to reek of urine.

Each time a dog eliminates in the wrong place, this habit becomes harder to change. The dog smells its urine just about everywhere, which makes one spot seem as good as another to pee. This problem can become much worse if the dog is also using its urine to intentionally mark objects in the house. Again, the amount of urine voided is so small with toy breeds that owners often don't realize the extent of the problem until it has become a firm habit.

Because toy dogs' small size leads to small accidents, owners may need to be extra-vigilant with a toy breed.

Addressing the Needs of Toy Breeds

The best solution is to limit the area in which the dog is allowed to roam. Baby-gates can keep the little piddler in the same room with you, so you can maintain a close watch. You might leash your pup to your belt so it has to stay right with you. That way you won't miss its body signals when it has to eliminate.

For a minimum of three weeks, you must not allow your pup to make its old mistakes. It will take at least that long for eliminating in the correct area to become the dog's new habit. When you cannot watch your pup like a hawk, either crate it or confine it to its puppy corral with papers on the floor.

Everything about toy dogs is in miniature except their intellect and determination. Little dogs are very bright, but can cling as stubbornly as a giant to bad habits. Repetition of the correct elimination behavior and praise for success are the keys to stopping potty accidents in toy dogs.

Health - Related
Problems

Not all potty problems are behaviorally based. There are a number of health-related reasons a dog might be unable to maintain elimination cleanliness. Some of these problems are inherited, some are infectious and some are caused by environmental factors.

Many health-related elimination problems can be helped or cured with proper treatment. Delayed medical care can cause great suffering and possibly result in the dog's death. If your dog is having problems controlling its bowels or bladder, before you assume that it's soiling deliberately, take it to the veterinarian for a thorough health check.

How a Dog's Elimination System Works

A dog's elimination system is closely allied with its digestive and reproductive systems. A disease or abnormality in any of these three systems may cause or worsen problems in the other two. Dog owners sometimes become frustrated with persistent housetraining problems and punish the dog without realizing that the trouble has a physical cause. It's unfair to blame a dog for potty accidents that it can't control. To avoid misunderstandings, it will help to understand how your dog's body works.

The digestive system processes foods and liquids the dog consumes, then moves the wastes out of the body through the intestinal and urinary systems. Both male and female bodies digest food and eliminate solid waste the same way, but anatomical and hormonal differences between the sexes influence the workings of their urinary systems.

URINARY SYSTEM

A normal dog of either sex has two kidneys, each with a narrow ureter tube leading to a bladder from which another tube, the urethra, carries urine to the outside. The kidneys filter out toxins from the dog's body and excrete them in the urine. The two ureters transport urine from the kidneys to the bladder, where it is held until passed through the urethra during urination.

Some urinary problems affect both sexes while others are common in one gender but not the other. Neutering can effect both male and female urinary conditions with hormonal causes.

Males

In male dogs the outside opening of the urethra is at the tip of the penis. The male's urethra is relatively long and narrow. The prostate gland surrounds the urethra at the base of the bladder.

Females

The female's urethra is shorter but wider in diameter than the male's. The urethra exits the female's body through the vaginal opening. There is no prostate gland in the female.

Urinary Incontinence

Voluntary urination involves muscles in the bladder wall, valves in the urethra and abdominal pressure. Urinary incontinence is the inability to control the voluntary passage of urine from the body. There are a number of possible causes.

STRUCTURALLY BASED URINARY INCONTINENCE

The urethral valves normally prevent leakage between urinations. Incomplete or weak urethral valves are one cause of incontinence. A nerve pinched between vertebrae can be another cause. Males can become incontinent, particularly from prostate problems, but incontinence is much more common in females.

Urinary incontinence is seen in both male and female dogs, but is much more prevalent in females.

Most at risk are medium- to large-sized bitches. Some have an abnormally positioned bladder with a shorter than normal urethra. Others have a structural abnormality that allows urine to pool in the vagina.

HORMONALLY BASED URINARY INCONTINENCE

By far, the most common cause of urinary incontinence in bitches is a low blood level of the hormone estrogen. Ninety percent of bitches with urinary incontinence have been spayed, and half of those develop the problem within one year after spaying. Some researchers warn against early spaying for this reason, but bitches spayed after maturity can also develop estrogen-related urinary incontinence.

Symptoms of Urinary Incontinence

Urinary incontinence does not manifest itself the same way in every dog that has it. The dog may void urine without being aware that it has done so. This can happen while awake or asleep. In some, there is a continuous dribbling of urine. In others, the escape of urine is intermittent and related to a rise in pressure inside the bladder, as when the dog coughs or sneezes, jumps, lies down or becomes excited.

If a pup seems very difficult to housetrain, or a dog that has been trained for some time has urination accidents, it may be ill and need veterinary attention. A great wrong is done when owners, frustrated by a dog's uncontrolled urination, punish the dog for breaking housetraining. Before you get angry with your dog about uncontrolled peeing, take it to the doctor to rule out physical problems. A dog with a physical cause for incontinence may be helped through proper medication, but punishment will not help at all.

Treatment and Aftercare for Urinary Incontinence

To determine the cause of a dog's incontinence, the veterinarian will carry out a complete physical exam. This usually includes genital and rectal examinations, urinalysis, x-ray and ultrasound. Once the cause has been identified, treatment will begin.

If the incontinence is caused by an abnormally positioned bladder, the veterinarian will surgically correct it. Hormonal imbalance will be treated with estrogen in bitches or testosterone in males. Medication may also be prescribed to improve the urethral seal.

Aftercare involves administering the prescribed medication. If the dog does not respond to medication, care involves keeping it clean, dry and as comfortable as possible. Trim the hair close around the genital area so urine evaporates quickly and doesn't burn the dog's skin. Petroleum jelly smeared over the genital area will further protect from the irritation of constant wetness.

INCONTINENCE DURING SLEEP

A dog that urinates in its sleep will need special care paid to its bedding. It must be kept clean and dry, or both the bedding and dog will smell terrible. A synthetic fleece pad atop newspapers or diapers makes a good washable bed for an incontinent dog. Urine can seep through the fleece into the absorbent material below so the dog remains as dry as possible. A sheet of plastic under the dog's bed will keep urine from soaking through to the floor.

Dogs that suffer from incontinence while asleep will need special bedding.

Conditions Affecting Urination

Excessive or uncontrollable urination is a symptom of several health problems. If your pup or dog seems to pee a lot, or if it's over 4 months old and still difficult to house-train, have your veterinarian check for health-related causes.

Do not delay a health check. Severe kidney damage can result from relatively minor infections. When kidneys are harmed badly enough they may shut down. Urination problems are not only messy and annoying, they can become life-threatening.

CYSTITIS AND URINARY TRACT INFECTIONS

Cystitis is an inflammation of the internal lining of the bladder. The usual cause is infection by bacteria that enter the bladder through the urethra. Cystitis is more common in females than in males because the female urethra provides a shorter, easier path to the bladder for bacteria.

In both sexes, the urethra normally has bacteria in it from outside contamination. If everything functions properly, the bacteria is washed away by urine when the bladder is emptied. It is important that a dog urinates frequently enough to keep bacteria flushed out before they migrate up the urethra. Once inside the bladder, bacteria can cause infection and inflammation of the bladder lining. An infection of the bladder can lead to severe kidney disease.

THE IMPORTANCE OF WATER

Water is the elixir of life. All living creatures need water to survive. A dog should be allowed as much fresh water as it wants to drink. To digest food and to excrete wastes, a dog needs water. To prevent dehydration, low blood pressure and life-threatening shock, a dog needs water.

Decreasing the daily water intake was used in times past during housetraining to control a pup's need to urinate. We now know this is a very unhealthy idea. Without sufficient water, a pup may get cystitis, which can make housetraining nearly impossible. Free access to water is the prevention and a major part of the cure for several conditions causing uncontrolled urination. Plenty of water to drink and plenty of opportunity to urinate will keep a pup healthy and accomplish housetraining more quickly.

Anything that causes a dog to urinate less frequently than normal can put it at risk for developing cystitis. Two common causes of cystitis are insufficient drinking water and insufficient opportunity to urinate, both of which are under the dog owner's control.

Symptoms of Cystitis

You may suspect cystitis if your dog voids small amounts of urine at frequent intervals. (This is not the same as marking behavior in which urine is "rationed" in small quantities to mark scent posts.) With cystitis, a dog will experience discomfort when urinating. Males that normally lift a leg to pee may squat instead. There may be a tinge of blood in the urine, and the dog may have pain in its abdomen.

Cystitis can cause a dog to urinate indoors, even when it has been completely housetrained. The dog is so uncomfortable when it urinates that, trying to find some way to void without pain, the dog seeks the comfort of its master's presence. A dog with cystitis, looking for a less painful place to urinate, may wet on your couch or bed, or in its own bed. This behavior shocks and distresses owners, and some jump to the conclusion that the dog is soiling willfully. The mistaken owner then punishes the unfortunate pup instead of seeking the medical care it needs to recover. Cystitis is a painful condition, but it usually responds well to early treatment.

Treatment and Aftercare for Cystitis

In the early stages, a bladder infection will usually clear up quickly with a round of antibiotics. Persistent infections may require longer treatment. The owner should encourage a dog recovering from cystitis to drink plenty of water.

Change the dog's drinking water several times a day to keep it fresh and appetizing. That alone will encourage most dogs to drink more freely. It is important to check with the doctor before adding salt to your dog's food.

Give your dog an opportunity to urinate frequently. Do not force it to hold its urine while it waits at home for you all day. When you are not there to let your dog out, give it access to a fenced area through a pet door, or train it to go indoors on paper. Holding its urine very long is bad for the dog's health and can cause cystitis in and of itself. To prevent or to recover from this condition, a dog needs plenty of fluid intake and output.

A dog with cystitis may soil your bed or couch, looking for a place to urinate without pain.

UROLITHIASIS

Uroliths are mineral "stones" that can form in the urinary system. They are most often found in the bladder, but may move to the urethra and, if too large to pass, become lodged there. Most uroliths are struvite (magnesium ammonium phosphate). Others contain cystine, urate or oxalate as the main ingredient. Different types of uroliths are treated with different medications and procedures, but all can cause pain and problems with urination.

Any age dog can have problems with uroliths, but they are most common between the ages of 4 and 6 years. Male dogs have more troubles with uroliths than females because the longer, narrower male urethra tends to trap the stones. In serious cases, uroliths can completely block the urethra, preventing urine from passing. This can lead to sudden kidney failure and death.

Breeds at Higher Risk

Several breeds of dogs have a higher than average incidence of urolithiasis. They are the Cocker Spaniel, Dachshund, Dalmatian, Miniature Poodle, Shih Tzu and Yorkshire Terrier. Dogs of these breeds may inherit a body chemistry that predisposes them to form certain types of uroliths.

Symptoms of Urolithiasis

The symptoms of urolithiasis are similar to those of cystitis. The dog may become incontinent or it may have difficulty urinating or experience discomfort toward the end of urination. A dog with urolithiasis may strain to urinate, especially a male with stones blocking the urethra. Urine may be tinged with blood. Complete blockage will cause cessation of urination, which, left untreated, soon leads to death.

Dalmatians are one of several breeds with a relatively high incidence of urolithiasis.

Treatment and Aftercare of Urolithiasis

When the veterinarian examines a dog for urolithiasis, he or she will palpate the abdomen, take a urine sample, may x-ray the urinary system and may put a catheter up the urethra to locate the blockage. Some veterinarians will also perform an ultrasound exam of the dog's abdomen.

It is important that the doctor determine exactly which kind of uroliths the dog has. The various types are treated differently, depending on their mineral ingredients. Struvite or urate uroliths can be dissolved with a special diet or medication that affects the chemistry of the urine. Oxalate or cystine uroliths will not dissolve and must be surgically removed. Antibiotics are often prescribed in urolithiasis to treat associated urinary tract infections.

Your veterinarian will instruct you on administering the prescribed medication and special diet for a dog with uroliths. The medication dissolves uroliths the dog currently has, and the special diet helps prevent new stones from forming.

A dog that has had stones must always be allowed access to plenty of fresh drinking water. The dog's water intake must be sufficient so it can flush mineral crystals out of the bladder before they build into uroliths. It is very important that the dog have plenty of water and opportunity to urinate as often as it needs. A dog forced to hold its urine for long periods may form bladder stones.

Some veterinarians recommend increased salt intake for certain urolithiasis patients. The purpose of adding salt is to increase the dog's thirst and water consumption. This is not the proper treatment for every case, however, so do not add salt to your dog's diet unless your veterinarian says it is indicated for your dog's condition.

CHRONIC RENAL (KIDNEY) FAILURE

The kidneys are vital to remove toxins from the body. When they cannot do this job, the dog becomes very ill. Long-term kidney infections, left untreated, will eventually cause renal failure. Congenital defects and cancer may also cause the kidneys to fail. Renal failure is very serious and may cause death if intervention is not swift.

Any dog may be at risk for chronic renal failure, but symptoms generally do not appear until a dog is over 5 years of age.

Symptoms of Chronic Renal Failure

When the kidneys fail, they become unable to concentrate fluid wastes, so there is an excessive volume of urine voided. To compensate for water loss, the dog may be very thirsty and drink more than usual. A dog in chronic renal failure will be generally ill and debilitated. It may vomit or have diarrhea, its breath will smell bad from its toxic internal condition, it may have little appetite and may lose weight. It may also become anemic and develop bone abnormalities. The dog will appear depressed both physically and mentally.

Symptoms do not always show that a dog is experiencing this condition. A dog in chronic renal failure can appear normal until, suddenly, its kidneys shut down. This puts the dog into life-threatening acute renal failure.

Treatment and Aftercare for Chronic Renal Failure

When a veterinarian diagnoses chronic renal failure, the dog will be placed on medication to correct its body chemistry imbalance and to control symptoms. The dog must also be fed a restricted or prescription diet, to ease the load on its kidneys.

When the dog has recovered, it will still be fragile. It will need to stay rested and warm, and all stress should be avoided. You and your veterinarian will monitor your dog's progress by keeping close track of its weight. You may also be asked to record your dog's food and water intake and urine output.

ENDOCRINE (HORMONAL) DISORDERS

The endocrine system uses the blood stream to transport hormones. Hormones produced within the endocrine system affect production and use of other hormones and body chemicals. Endocrine disorders can cause elimination problems. Often a dog's inability to control its elimination causes owners to take it to the veterinarian. Endocrine disorders may be discovered this way, allowing proper treatment to begin.

ADRENAL HORMONE DISORDERS

Two causes of urination problems result from abnormal production of adrenal hormones. Cushing's disease (hyperadrenocorticism) is due to an overabundance of adrenal hormones. Addison's disease (hypoadrenocorticism) is the opposite, an adrenal hormone deficiency. Either will cause elimination problems.

Cushing's Disease (Hyperadrenocorticism)

Cushing's disease is also called Cushing's syndrome. When this disease occurs, the adrenal glands atop the kidneys produce too much cortisol (a form of cortisone). The most common cause is a pituitary brain tumor that secretes adrenocorticotropic hormone (ACTH) in large amounts. The ACTH stimulates the adrenals to overproduce cortisol. Another cause of Cushing's disease might be a tumor in the adrenal gland that causes it to secrete extra cortisol.

At risk for Cushing's disease are dogs that have been treated with corticosteroids. These drugs are often prescribed for dogs with allergies and inflammatory conditions. This type is referred to as iatrogenic (meaning "doctor-caused") Cushing's disease.

Several breeds have a hereditary tendency to develop hyperadrenocorticism. They are the Boxer, Boston Terrier, Dachshund and Poodle.

Symptoms of Cushing's Disease

Increased thirst and increased urination are common symptoms of Cushing's disease. Increased hunger is another symptom for many dogs with this illness. The excess water and food the dog takes in make it have to eliminate more. Another symptom, muscular weakness, causes a dog trouble holding its bladder and bowels. The dog will unavoidably break housetraining if it can't reach its potty area in time.

You may see increased thirst and increased hunger in a dog with Cushing's disease.

Other symptoms of Cushing's disease are symmetrical hair loss on both sides of the body, high blood pressure, thinning of the skin, fat deposits in the liver, calcium deposits in the skin and plugged hair follicles on the underside. Many dogs diagnosed with Cushing's disease also have a history of recurring urinary tract infections.

Diagnosis can be difficult with this disease, sometimes requiring analysis of numerous blood samples.

Treatment and Aftercare of Cushing's Disease

Medication is the treatment most veterinarians choose for dogs with this disease. One medicine works by poisoning the affected adrenal gland so it cannot produce such excessive levels of cortisol. A different medication, which inhibits steroid formation, is used for the pituitary-dependent form of Cushing's disease. Even when the cause of Cushing's disease is a tumor, most cases are not treated surgically because of dangers to the dog.

A dog diagnosed with Cushing's disease must remain on medication for the rest of its life to control this condition. The dog must frequently be retested to be certain it's still on the correct dosage as its body adapts to the medicine.

Addison's Disease (Hypoadrenocorticism)

Addison's disease is fairly rare, and most cases are the result of an atrophy of the adrenal gland. Addison's disease is the opposite condition from Cushing's. Cortisol production is deficient instead of overabundant. In Addison's disease, cortisol production is not the only problem, however, because other adrenal hormones also will be insufficiently produced. Addison's disease can be fatal, because dogs can't survive without adrenal hormones.

Two iatrogenic ("doctor-caused") forms of Addison's disease may occur in dogs with adrenal damage from having been overtreated with certain medications. One type is caused by overtreatment with corticosteroids for inflammatory conditions. Some of these patients recover after awhile if the medicine is withdrawn, but in others, the damage to the adrenals is permanent.

The other form of iatrogenic Addison's disease can occur in Cushing's disease patients overtreated with a drug used to control cortisol overproduction. In this form of Addison's disease, damage to the adrenals is permanent.

Symptoms of Addison's Disease

Depression is often the first symptom of Addison's disease. The dog may be weak, have little energy, and become anemic. Appetite may be diminished and the dog may lose weight from not eating enough. It may also vomit and have loose stools. Some dogs with Addison's disease drink and urinate a lot. An important clinical sign of Addison's disease is that the symptoms tend to come and go.

Treatment and Aftercare of Addison's Disease

Diagnosis of Addison's disease involves blood tests to check levels of the chemicals produced by different organs. Because this disease is potentially life-threatening, treatment may begin before test results confirm the diagnosis.

Dogs with this disease may have very low blood pressure and abnormal electrolyte levels. These are serious symptoms that can cause shock and death. Both these problems can be helped by increasing fluid intake. Rehydration therapy is started immediately, even before beginning to treat the adrenal problem.

To treat Addison's disease, the patient is administered the hormones it is unable to produce. Cortisone is the easiest to replace; low doses of the drug prednisone are used for this. The adrenally produced mineralcorticoids are more difficult to replace. These hormones normally regulate production of electrolytes, without which the body is unable to function. The medications for this can be given orally on a daily basis, injected monthly or implanted under the skin in pellet form every ten months. A dog must be retested periodically to assure proper dosage.

DIABETES MELLITUS

Diabetes mellitus is a condition in which the dog has higher than normal blood glucose levels. Insulin produced by the pancreas normally controls the amount of glucose sugar in the blood. With diabetes, either there is not enough insulin being produced or the body tissues do not respond properly to it.

Dogs at risk for developing diabetes are usually over 8 years old, although the disease has occasionally been diagnosed in pups under a year. Obese dogs are more likely to become diabetic than those of normal weight. At highest risk are unspayed bitches.

Breeds at Higher Risk

Certain breeds have a higher incidence of diabetes than others. Among the breeds with an inherited

tendency for diabetes are the Cocker and Cavalier King Charles Spaniels, Dachshund, Doberman Pinscher, German Shepherd Dog, Golden Retriever, Labrador Retriever, Pomeranian, Rottweiler and Samoyed.

If your dog received genes from one or more of these breeds and starts to show any symptoms of diabetes, have it examined by a veterinarian immediately. The sooner treatment for diabetes is begun, the less damage will be done by the disease.

Symptoms of Diabetes Mellitus

Increased thirst and appetite are common early symptoms of diabetes.

Obesity puts a dog at risk for contracting diabetes, so make an effort to keep your dog trim.

Even with an increase in appetite, however, there may be a loss of weight. A dog with diabetes will often have a poor coat. Cataracts can also be caused by diabetes.

A dog with diabetes will pass greater than normal quantities of urine. With diabetes, the bladder fills more quickly than normal. A dog cannot help urinating when its bladder reaches maximum capacity and the diabetic dog may have accidents at night or when shut inside without access to its elimination area.

When a dog first starts having accidents, owners may view its urination as a behavior problem and punish the dog or try harder to train it. This is useless, because the dog is sick and cannot help itself. If your housetrained adult dog suddenly begins peeing in the house at night or when left alone, take it to the veterinarian right away to check for a physical cause.

Advanced cases of diabetes exhibit alarming symptoms. The dog will act depressed, will breathe rapidly and may vomit. Eventually, an untreated diabetic dog will stop passing urine altogether. Shortly after that, it may go into a coma and die. Diabetes mellitus is nothing to fool around with. If you have any reason at all to suspect it, take your dog in to be checked.

Treatment and Aftercare for Diabetes

Diabetes is a serious condition that requires special care. The dog's diet must be monitored and it may need to be given daily injections of insulin. Diabetes mellitus is not a condition that will go away by itself, it must be treated. Left untreated, diabetes can kill.

When a veterinarian checks for diabetes, he or she will first give the dog a thorough physical examination that will include laboratory analysis of both blood and urine. The doctor may also x-ray the dog and/or do an ultrasound exam to look for structural abnormalities.

If high blood glucose levels are found, the veterinarian will start your dog on medications to help its body function more normally. The dog may need to be hospitalized for a few days to stabilize its condition. It will probably require daily insulin injections for the rest of its life to manage this disease. Your veterinarian will teach you how to medicate your dog. Absolute consistency with medications will be vital, as slipups can cause misery or even death.

Dietary modification is important in the treatment and care of diabetes. If the dog is obese, its weight must be reduced. The veterinarian may place the dog on a prescription diet or recommend other foods. Stick with this regimen. Don't change the diet or give tidbits or treats unless the doctor specifically tells you it's permissible. Because a diabetic dog's blood sugar level depends on regular feedings, you must be vigilant in keeping to the dog's feeding schedule. All dogs should be exercised daily and diabetic dogs are no exception.

Exercise should be moderate, however. Strenuous bouts of activity must be avoided as they could cause a blood sugar imbalance to occur.

Not every dog owner is able to give a diabetic dog the care it needs. Your veterinarian will discuss with you what steps will be necessary for your diabetic dog to maintain a relatively healthy and comfortable life. Diabetes doesn't go away and must be closely managed every day, but with proper medication and care a dog with diabetes can live a happy life.

PROSTATE GLAND DISORDERS

Neutering a male dog can signifi-cantly lower its chances of prostate disorders and the resulting urinary problems.

The prostate gland surrounds the male's urethra at the neck of the bladder. (Females have no prostate gland.) If the gland becomes enlarged, it presses on the urethra and can cause urinary problems. The two conditions that most frequently cause this are prostatitis and prostate hyperplasia. Tumors, cysts or abscesses of the

prostate may also cause urinary problems. Neutering a male dog lowers its risk of prostate disorders.

Prostatitis is an inflammation of the prostate gland, generally caused by bacteria from the urinary system. This can be very painful for the dog.

Prostate hyperplasia is not a painful condition, but it can cause urinary incontinence. Hyperplasia of the prostate occurs only in intact (unneutered) males. It most often shows up between the ages of 6 and 10 years.

Symptoms of Prostate Gland Disorders
Incontinence is a symptom of prostate disorders, and there may be blood in the urine. Blood or pus may be passed from the dog's penis at times other than urination. The dog may strain to urinate or defecate. He may be constipated or pass ribbon-like feces.

Treatment and Aftercare of Prostate Disorders
The veterinarian will examine your dog thoroughly, including abdominal palpation, a rectal exam and urethral

catheterization to obtain samples for analysis. The vet may also use x-rays, ultrasound or biopsy to diagnose the cause of the disorder.

If the problem is a tumor, cyst or abscess, surgery will be performed to remove the growth and probably the prostate gland itself. If the trouble is prostatitis, antibiotics will often take care of it, but castration may also be necessary. With hyperplasia, castration is often needed, although hormones or other medication may help.

Bowel Problems

Normally, the large intestine absorbs moisture back from the feces before defecation. This way, the stool is well-formed and excess water is not lost from the body. There are numerous causes of bowel problems and the most common symptom is diarrhea.

DIARRHEA

When anything causes the large intestine to absorb inadequate amounts of water, too much fluid will be excreted with the feces. The feces will be loose or watery, and bowel movements will be impossible for the dog to control. This is diarrhea, which is sometimes the reason for housetraining lapses. Diarrhea can have many causes, including structural abnormalities, parasites and disease.

Dehydration

Diarrhea isn't just uncomfortable and messy, it can actually be very dangerous if it leads to dehydration. Dehydration results from excess water being lost through diarrhea, vomiting or excessive urination. This can cause

---

GIVING MEDICINE TO YOUR DOG

It's easy to medicate a dog if you know the techniques.

Liquid Medicine. Check first to find out if your dog likes the taste. Put a drop on the end of your finger and offer it to your dog. If it licks it off, try a second drop. If the dog will lick medicine off your finger twice, it will probably lap up the dosage from a bowl.

If your dog doesn't like the flavor, you'll have to use "Plan B." Put the dose in a spoon or a needle-less syringe (ask your veterinarian for one). Pull out the corner of the dog's lip to form a pocket and pour the medicine into it. Then immediately tilt the dog's head up and gently stroke its throat until it swallows.

Pills. If your dog has any appetite, you may be able to slip it a pill hidden in some tasty food. Processed cheese works well, or any food that your dog will gulp greedily that's sticky enough to hold a pill until it's been swallowed. Ask your veterinarian if the food in which you plan to "hide" the medication is healthy for your dog.

other body systems to malfunction. Dehydration causes a lowered blood volume, which can lead to fatal shock. If your dog has a very loose stool and/or is vomiting, watch carefully that it doesn't become dehydrated.

CHRONIC LIVER DISEASE

The liver is an important organ for maintaining the health of the entire body. It produces blood proteins, converts waste products into substances the kidneys can excrete, processes and stores fats and carbohydrates, produces bile for digestion and purifies the blood. With all those duties, it's no wonder a dog suffers if its liver is not functioning properly.

Older dogs are at risk for chronic liver disease, as are pups with congenital abnormalities of the organ. Common causes of liver disease are immune system or bile duct disorders, long-term inflammation or cancer.

To diagnose liver disorders, the veterinarian will perform blood and urine tests, analyze abdominal fluid buildup and may use x-rays or ultrasound. Sometimes the best way to determine the cause of liver problems is through biopsy or exploratory surgery.

Older dogs are at risk for chronic liver disease.

A breed at higher risk for liver disorder is the Bedlington Terrier. In Bedlington Terriers, a hereditary condition known as copper toxicosis causes chronic liver disease. About 25 percent of Bedlingtons are afflicted with this disease, 50 percent more carry the gene but are not afflicted and only 25 percent are free of the gene.

Symptoms of Chronic Liver Disease

Diarrhea is a common symptom of liver disease. Excessive thirst is another, and this may cause excessive urination. The dog may not want to eat and will lose weight as a result. There may be also be vomiting and abdominal swelling. A dog with liver disease will have very low energy.

Treatment for Chronic Liver Disease

There is no cure for chronic liver disease, but its progress can be slowed. The dog should be kept as free of stress as much as is possible. It will need a special diet and plenty of rest. The veterinarian can prescribe medication to reduce fluid in the dog's abdomen and, possibly, antibiotics for specific causes. Tragically, even with excellent care, a diseased liver will continue to deteriorate.

PARASITES

Parasites can cause chronic or acute problems with elimination. If your dog's bowel movements are very loose, tinged with blood or have an especially foul odor, seek veterinary help.

Diagnosis of a specific parasite is necessary to prescribe proper treatment. Home remedies can be very dangerous. A favorite old-time "cure" for worms, tobacco, contains a potent nerve toxin that can miss the worms and badly sicken the dog. Over-the-counter remedies from the grocery or pet store are not always effective, and they can be dangerous if used improperly. Your veterinarian is the best person to decide which antiparasitic medicine will help your dog.

Worms

Worms that inhabit the intestines can cause bowel problems. Roundworms are common, especially in pups, and can cause diarrhea. Other common intestinal parasites that use canine hosts are hookworm, whipworm and tapeworm. Your veterinarian can test for worms by examining a fecal sample through a microscope. Some of these worms can afflict humans as well, so keep your dog free of worms for its sake and your own.

If you suspect your dog might have worms, or if you just haven't had it checked recently, take a small, fresh sample of its stool to the veterinary clinic. Within a short time, the technician can tell you if your dog has worms.

When giving your dog worm medicine, carefully follow your veterinarian's instructions or those on the product package. Your dog must be weighed to accurately calculate proper dosage. To weigh your dog, hold it while you weigh yourself, then weigh yourself again without the dog. Be sure to give only the dosage correct for its weight, as overmedicating with worming medicine can make a dog very ill.

Coccidia

Coccidia are microscopic parasites that are common in dogs but rarely cause a problem unless the animal is

Common internal parasites (l-r): roundworm, whipworm, tapeworm and hookworm.

under stress. Under these circumstances, the parasite can get a foothold and make a puppy miserable with copious mucous-laden diarrhea. At risk for coccidial infection are nursing or recently weaned pups, dogs with a weak immune system and those that have just moved to a new home. Because coccidiosis occurs with such relative frequency in dogs soon after changing homes, this is considered a stress-related problem.

Dogs infected with coccidia are usually treated with sulfa drugs. Good sanitation of the home or kennel environment is vital to protect against the spread of the parasite. Coccidia oocysts (eggs) can survive for years and are resistant to most disinfectants. On hard surfaces, ammonia compounds will kill the eggs and steam cleaning can remove them from fabrics and carpets.

Giardia

Giardia are protozoan parasites that are acquired by drinking water from streams contaminated with the microorganism. Giardia attack their host by attaching to the wall of the intestines without penetrating the cells. They reproduce there and are passed through the feces. It is not known if dogs and people can infect each other directly, but humans can contract giardia from the same water sources that dogs get it from.

Giardiasis is commonly found in dogs but doesn't always cause an overt problem. When it does, though, the dog will have diarrhea, which may occur over a short or long period of time. The stools are soft, pale and foul smelling. Some dogs will lose weight and condition.

Fecal examination is the method for diagnosing giardiasis. The common type of fecal exam often won't turn up this pest, so a special technique is used. If your dog is diagnosed with giardiasis, the veterinarian will prescribe medication to eliminate the parasites.

Common disinfectants, like chlorine bleach, can be used to kill giardia cysts in the dog's elimination area. This is important to avoid reinfection and to prevent the spread of the disease to other family members. If your dog has been diagnosed with giardiasis and you have any similar symptoms, have your physician test you for the organism.

Viral Diseases

Responsible breeders and owners make sure their pups are immunized for the common viral dog diseases. At greatest risk for viral disease are young pups and elderly dogs. In those groups, the immune system is not always as strong as it needs to be to ward off viruses. In most cases, a properly vaccinated dog will be immune, but some may still contract a disease.

Viral Diarrhea

Several viral diseases cause diarrhea (which may contain blood) and also vomiting, which can cause the patient to become dehydrated. These are distemper, parvovirus, coronavirus and leptospirosis. A pup with any of these diseases will look and act very ill. Viral disease can quickly debilitate a young pup, but a high percentage can be saved if they receive prompt veterinary treatment. If you suspect your dog has a viral disease, call your veterinary clinic immediately.

If your dog has diarrhea, it's important to keep its backside cleaned. Carefully trim the hair around and below the pup's anus so feces will not be caught there. If the dog's behind is very soiled, wash with water and dry it thoroughly. If soiling is light, disposable baby wipes will do the job.

Age-Related Problems

Some problems with elimination behavior are due to age-related physical causes. Training won't help these potty problems, but compassion and good care will.

INFANCY

Infancy is the most common age-related cause of elimination problems. Luckily, this is cured by time, and a healthy pup will mature with good bladder and bowel control. Until a pup is at least 4 months old, though, you really should expect it to have elimination accidents.

Young puppies lack the muscle control and the intellectual development needed to control their elimination— keep your expectations low.

A young puppy's muscles and organs are not mature enough to completely control elimination. Also, a pup doesn't always understand or remember the housetraining rules at first. This combination of physical immaturity and social ignorance makes some cleanup chores for you. Patience and consistency are the keys to housetraining. A good supply of paper towels won't hurt, either.

SENIOR YEARS

In its senior years, a dog may begin to lose strength in muscles that control elimination. Age-related incontinence due to decreased muscle control may occur either awake or asleep, depending on the cause. Never shame your old dog about this. It probably is already embarrassed that it couldn't control itself. Be patient and compassionate, your old buddy needs to know you care.

An older dog with incontinence should have a comfortable, washable bed. Synthetic fleece pads over top of absorbent washable or disposable materials will keep your dog out of its leaked urine. The bedding can be laundered as often as needed.

Don't Hesitate to Call Your Veterinarian

Considering all the physical problems that can cause a dog to break housetraining, it's amazing that any floor is ever dry and clean.

If your dog is slow to housetrain, has recurrent lapses in clean habits or suddenly breaks elimination rules, be sure to check for physical causes. It does absolutely no good to scold or punish a dog for wetting or messing when it cannot control itself. In some cases, the stress of scolding can actually worsen the dog's condition.

If you have any reason to suspect physical problems might be affecting housetraining, take your dog to a veterinarian right away. Early treatment can cure or control most health problems that cause elimination troubles.

part four

Beyond
the
Basics

Resources

Books
About Health Care

Ackerman, Lowell, DVM. *Owner's Guide to Dog Health*. Neptune, NJ: TFH Publications, 1995.

Carlson, Delbert G., DVM and James M. Giffin, MD. *Dog Owner's Home Veterinary Handbook*. New York: Howell Book House, 1992.

Evans, Mark. *Dog Doctor*. New York: Howell Book House, 1996.

Pitcairn, Richard H., DVM and Susan Hubble Pitcairn. *Natural Health for Dogs & Cats*. Emmaus, PA: Rodale Press, 1982.

Stein, Diane. *Natural Healing for Dogs & Cats*. Freedom, CA: The Crossing Press, 1993.

About Behavior

Coren, Stanley. *The Intelligence of Dogs*. New York: Bantam Books, 1994.

Dunbar, Ian, PhD, MRCVS. *Dog Behavior: An Owner's Guide to a Happy Healthy Pet*. New York: Howell Book House, 1999.

Fogle, Bruce, DVM, MRCVS. *The Dog's Mind*. New York: Howell Book House, 1990.

About Training

Benjamin, Carol Lea. *Mother Knows Best*. New York: Howell Book House, 1985.

Morn, September B. *Dogs Love To Please*. Bellingham, WA: Pawprince Press, 1994.

———. *Crate-Den Training*. Bellingham, WA: Pawprince Press, 1995.

———. *Positive Potty Training*. Bellingham, WA: Pawprince Press, 1995.

Walkowicz, Chris and Bonnie Wilcox, DVM. *Old Dogs, Old Friends*. New York: Howell Book House, 1991.

Magazines

AKC GAZETTE: The Official Journal for the Sport of Purebred Dogs. American Kennel Club, 51 Madison Ave., New York, NY 10010.

Bloodlines Journal. United Kennel Club, 100 E. Kilgore Rd., Kalamazoo, MI 49001-5598.

DOG FANCY. Fancy Publications, P.O. Box 6050, Mission Viejo, CA 92690.

Dog World. 29 N. Wacker Dr., Chicago, IL 60606.

Videos

Carlson, Jeanne. *Good Puppy*. Sound Dog Productions, Inc., P.O. Box 27488, Seattle, WA 98125.

Dunbar, Ian, PhD, MRCVS. *SIRIUS Puppy Training*. James & Kenneth Publishers, 2140 Shattuck Ave., #2406, Berkeley, CA 94704.